GUMBOOT PRACTICE

GUMBOOT PRACTICE

Portrait of a Country Solicitor

John Francis

Illustrated by Ron Tiner

Smith Settle

First published in 1989 by
Smith Settle Ltd
Ilkley Road
Otley
West Yorkshire
LS21 3JP

Second Impression 1989
Third Impression 1989

ISBN Paperback 1 870071 38 7
Hardback 1 870071 39 5

Designed, printed and bound by
SMITH SETTLE
Ilkley Road, Otley, West Yorkshire LS21 3JP

Dedication

This book is dedicated to my mother, whose sacrifices made it possible for me to pursue a career as a country solicitor, to my wife and family who have supported me throughout and encouraged me to write about it, and to my partners, staff and clients, past and present.

Author's Note

This book, which is part autobiography, part fact, part fiction and part pure fantasy, contains references to a number of real Yorkshire place names. The reader will not be able to find Denley on any map, for it is an amalgam of the different small towns and villages in which I have practised as a country solicitor. Most of the characters and clients described are composites or wholly imaginary too, and some of my boyhood recollections may have been distorted slightly by the passage of time.

I take this opportunity of gratefully acknowledging the various lawyers, poets, writers, naturalists and sportsmen whom I have quoted in the book.

Contents

An Articled Clerk I Soon Became

Yorkshire Boyhood

I knew two things about myself from an early age, the first was that I wanted to be a solicitor and the second that I wanted to be a country solicitor.

I was twelve years old when I was introduced to an old Yorkshire solicitor whose tweed suit, pipe and gravelly Yorkshire accent immediately reminded me of J B Priestley. On being told of my ambition to enter the legal profession he said, 'Well, lad, if tha wants to be a lawyer tha'll mek thy bread and butter and wi' luck a bit o' jam on top.' Over a quarter of a century later I still live in hope of that bit of jam!

I have always thought that twelve is a marvellous age for a boy. It is before the awkward and painful years of adolescence, before girls and parties, and before real worries of finding a job in life start to set in. At that age you also think yourself immortal. Amongst my generation of schoolboys 1953 was undoubtedly the 'annus mirabilis'. It was the Coronation year, the year Everest was conquered and the year of the Matthews' Cup Final. Most important of all for a Yorkshire boy it was also the year we won back the Ashes from Australia.

At that age I spent most of my time playing football or cricket with my friends and family. Epic 'cup finals' and 'test matches' were played in back garden, street, field, beach or any suitable - or as was usually the case totally unsuitable - piece of ground. What I really wanted to do when I was twelve was to dribble a football like Stanley Matthews or head it like Nat Lofthouse, to play an off drive like Len Hutton or a sweep like Dennis Compton.

Apart from football and cricket I had a go at and enjoyed most other sports, particularly the racquet games. I also began to develop what was to become an abiding love of natural history, country lore and country folk. When I was not playing football or cricket I was out in the countryside biking, fishing, collecting butterflies or just walking and exploring. Mine was a world of grazed knees, muddy clothes and Dandelion and Burdock. I didn't spend much time indoors. Me at twelve would have thought me at forty-five a very boring person, spending so much time in a stuffy office.

In those days a boy could roam at will in the countryside, and with the invaluable and generous encouragement given to me by various farmers, gardeners, keepers, sportsmen and naturalists who put up with my quest for knowledge, I soon started to learn. I learnt about farms and about stock, I learnt how to fish, how to catch rabbits, how to hunt and how to shoot.

I also learnt how to tend a garden and how to grow fruit and vegetables. I remember with particular affection and gratitude the farmers and allotment holders who took me under their wing. The former taught me how to hand-milk, how to make hay and how

1

to drive a tractor and ride a horse; the latter made me realise that whereas a suburban garden is for appearance, a country garden is for pleasure and for the kitchen.

I knew and loved those special, magic places I had discovered on my country rambles. The woods where there were still red squirrels and carpets of bluebells and wood anemones; the meadows where small skipper butterflies frolicked with common blues and small coppers among harebells and birdsfoot trefoil; the ponds which housed yellow-underbellied newts and dragonflies; the heather moors where I listened to the cry of the curlew, that harbinger of our northern spring; and my special field by the river full of cowslips and lady's smocks where I always saw the first orange-tip butterflies in early May. I soon knew all the Latin as well as English names of every British butterfly and I acquired a small knowledge of botany and ornithology. I was always acutely conscious, however, of how much in the world of nature there was to see, explore, understand and to learn.

I look back on my Yorkshire boyhood with the greatest possible pleasure and affection, tinged with a nostalgic regret that the sort of boyhood freedom I enjoyed can no longer be safely experienced by today's generation. I fear those days are gone forever. So, heigh-ho for the first trout I caught at Hayburn Wyke, for the dark green fritillaries I chased at Harwood Dale, for blackberrying at the reservoir and bilberrying near the crag, for the games we all played - tig, burglars and policemen, kick the can, marbles, skittles, hopscotch and conkers (and all the varied schoolboy preparations to make your conker invincible, which never seemed to work); and heigh-ho for the smell of the damp oak woods where we collected acorns, for glorious runs with the beagles, for tennis tournaments in summer when it always seemed to rain, for skating on the tarn when the frost held, for marvellous family parties, summer holidays at Filey, traditional Christmases and simple cosy evenings by an open fire, for climbing trees and picking fruit from the old gnarled trees in the orchard, but above all for the love, laughter and friendship of family and friends.

Today's children have television, computers and video games - indeed every type of fancy gadgetry which money can buy. For myself I would gladly exchange all those for a bike, a fishing rod, a butterfly net, a leather football and a cricket bat. But if I could have none of these things I would choose my old wireless set, from which I am sure I learnt just as much as I did at school. Who of my generation can forget *Uncle Mac, Paul Temple, Dick Barton, Journey into Space, The Archers* and all those marvellous serials which brought the classics to life.

As I listened to *Grand Hotel* and the orchestra's signature tune *Roses from the South*, I pictured myself in the Palm Court at Eastbourne, and Friday night was of course *Music Night*. This was the great age of radio comedy: *Ray's a Laugh, Take it from Here, The Goon Show, Educating Archie, Much-binding-in-the-Marsh* and *Life with the Lyons*. I loved listening to *Any Questions* with dear old Freddy Grisewood in the chair, and remember thinking that those two splendid countrymen, Ralph Wightman and A G Street, talked a good deal more sense than any of the politicians. *Sports Report* was a must, as was tuning in during the early hours to hear how England were getting on in Australia. There is also nothing like a good radio play for stimulating the imaginat. and when I went to bed and turned on the wireless my mind was opened up a. stimulated in a way which hours of watching television surely cannot do.

The wireless also played a significant part in my choice of career. One of my favourite programmes was the reconstruction of famous trials, particularly murder trials, by Edgar Lustgarten. This in turn caused me to start reading about the lives and cases of famous lawyers like Marshall Hall and Norman Birkett. Soon I knew nearly all their famous cases by heart.

At school I added to my interest in books by taking part in every kind of play, debate, discussion and argument. I later took up amateur dramatics, which was to prove an ideal preparation for the drama and theatre of the courtroom. I am sure it is a distinct advantage for a lawyer, or for a parson or an MP for that matter, to be a good actor!

I knew, then, before going away to public school - before my football and cricket playing, butterfly collecting prep school days were over - that I wanted to be a solicitor. I knew, however, that I wanted to practise law among my own people and within my own territory. Not for me the bright lights of the city, the commercial world or acting for property speculators or business tycoons. I wanted to be a country solicitor.

My Kind of Town

As a boy I was lucky to get to know many of the characters in Denley, the market town where I was destined to practise law. I was born there and brought up in a village only a few miles away. I grew up amongst the farmers who came to the two cattle markets in the town, the stallholders in the Friday market, the gardeners in their allotments, the keepers on the moors overlooking the town and above all the small shopkeepers - most of whom have now sadly disappeared or been replaced by supermarkets.

There was Alice Harbottle, she of white hair and pink cheeks, who generously presided over all those desirable and magical jars of goodies in her 'Olde Sweet Shoppe'; Ivor Westgate who bought baby budgerigars from children including a very pretty and charming girl called Rosemary from the same village as me, and who was later to become my wife; Joseph Jackson, miraculous craftsman in leather goods who supplied and mended our school satchels; and there was Edgar Wilkinson, who used to restring my tennis racquet and would invariably remark as he proudly handed it back to me, 'It's screamin' tight, lad, it's screamin' tight.'

Above all there was Fossets, the family grocers who justifiably claimed to be 'the shop which serves the district'. Whenever I think of Fossets I remember the friendly manager in brown overalls standing behind the counter - always with a pencil behind his ear - who used to greet me with a snatch of the popular song 'If I knew you were coming, I'd have baked a cake'. I remember too with almost tangible nostalgia their fine array of cheeses and the smell of freshly ground coffee.

The Jubilee Clock and the Buttercross right in the centre of town seemed to be where everything happened in Denley. In the old days this was where the Irish labourers were hired for the outlying farms in spring, where the gypsy dancing girl performed with her tambourine and where the farmers on market day Fridays used to bring their butter and baby chicks in cardboard boxes and leave them open to sell. The fluffy little chicks were forever tumbling out of the boxes and the farmers' wives would scoop them in again.

There were some splendid local characters in those days and one I remember with great affection was a gentleman tramp known to us boys as the 'Wild Man of Borneo'. Although of rather frightening appearance - for he was usually dressed in torn clothes and had a large bushy beard and bulbous red nose - he was perfectly harmless. He was wont to drop into the local shops where he would be treated like a lord, given a cup of tea and a bite to eat. In return he would give the shopkeeper a racing tip for the day, which would always be pinned to the front of his battered hat.

Apart from its small businesses and the characters which seemed to go with them, Denley was noted for its cinema known as 't' Scratchin' Shed' and its fine cricket and rugby clubs. It has always been said that there are more pubs and churches in Denley than in any other comparable place in Yorkshire. Church and chapel were deadly rivals in those days, evidenced amongst other things by their separate Whit Walks, but in the markets and the pubs the people came together and the talk was ever of sheep, cattle and produce, haytime and harvest, dogs and guns, shooting and fishing, and of course Leeds United and Yorkshire Cricket.

Like every good Tyke I had known five things about Yorkshire from birth. First, that Yorkshire (like Caesar's Gaul) was divided into three parts called Ridings, second that

there were more acres in Yorkshire than letters in the Bible, thirdly that the Pennines were there to protect us from Lancastrians, fourthly that you can always tell a Yorkshireman but you can't tell him much, and fifthly (and easily most important) that to be eligible to play for Yorkshire County Cricket Club you must be born within the county boundaries. Years later I had to educate my wife in this last matter when I insisted on a holiday being deferred to ensure that our first-born would, if a boy, be eligible to play for his county.

On the very top of the hill overlooking Denley stands a dilapidated folly built in Victorian times by an enlightened local landowner for the purely philanthropic motive of wishing to provide work for local unemployed labourers. Useless as a building it may have been but it was always a great place for Denley children to play 'hide and seek', 'murder in the dark' or just to explore. Here from the folly I would look out over what must be one of the finest views in all England. Immediately below me lay the town itself with its stone-built cottages, its markets, its pubs and its river; beyond it on the other side of the river climbed the heather moors, wild, mysterious, beautiful and in August ablaze with purple.

I knew then that Denley was my kind of town and that the farmers, traders and good Yorkshire folk who lived and worked there and in the surrounding villages were my kind of people, people whose lives and problems I wanted to share. But this was to think ahead, because I knew very well that I had a lot of learning to do first.

Mentors

If we are lucky, most of us at one time or another come under the influence of individuals outside the family who can teach us a lot about life. One of the mentors of my youth was old Jacob. He had been a farm labourer and countryman all his life and in his middle years he was employed by a major national company as a cattle-food salesman. He was undoubtedly one of the most successful salesmen that company employed, not because he was a brilliant salesman but because he could talk to the farmers like one of them. They trusted him implicitly and sought his advice on anything which went wrong on their farms, whether it was a sickly lamb, a crop which wasn't growing or a tractor which wouldn't start.

Moreover they were just as likely to take old Jacob's advice as that of a lawyer when it came to a boundary problem or dispute with a neighbour. Whatever the problem was, old Jacob always seemed able to 'fettle it', as he used to say, and the cattle food which he delivered to them in huge quantities was sold to them almost as an aside.

His tact and down-to-earth philosophy on such occasions would have done credit to any lawyer. I often think that he taught me much more about dealing with people - which is what being a solicitor is all about - than anything I learnt later at university or law school. I remember particularly one occasion when I went with Jacob to a farm where there had been a long-running dispute with a neighbouring farm over the maintainance of a boundary wall. Jacob, who knew both farmers, Bert and Charlie, well, got them together and walked the length of the wall, first up one side and then the other.

'Na then, Bert', he said, ' 'ow long 'ast tha known me?'

'About forty year. But what's that got to do wi' it?', replied Bert.

'An' 'ow about thee, Charlie, 'ow long 'ast thee known me?'

'I reckon about forty year an' all, Jacob', replied Charlie.

'An' 'ow long dos't tha both reckon yon wall 'as bin standin' 'ere?'

Bert and Charlie both looked at each other and scratched their heads.

'I'll tell thee both, shall I? It's bin theer sin' Adam were a lad, an' it'll still be standing many a year after all t' three on us is dead an' buried. If tha wants my opinion - an' if

not tha's gittin' it anyroad - life's too short for t' pair o' thee to waste time fratchin' ovver it. Na, cum on, let's settle t' job up an' git t' Dog an' Gun for a pint.'

Bert and Charlie hesitated for a moment, looked at each other cautiously and then said with one voice:

'Tha's reet, Jacob, life's too bloody short!'

A visit to a farm with old Jacob was an education in itself. He taught me to recognise the different breeds of sheep, pigs, cattle and poultry, about different types of agricultural machinery and how to tell whether the land was 'in good heart'. He also taught me not just to look at nature, the countryside and the wildlife it contained but to observe it. His motto for really seeing nature could have been 'more haste, less speed'. Or as he would more readily have put it: 'Tek it steady, lad, and tha'll 'appen see summat.'

There was one place which was a particular favourite of old Jacob's where he and I spent many happy hours together, and where I learnt from this wise old countryman the things that could not be gleaned from books or taught at school. To the passer-by this place cannot appear anything special, for to this day it looks like an ordinary area of boggy heathland grazed by sheep and cattle. Yet we both knew that we had only to get our gumboots out of the car, walk quietly into that heathland and within minutes we would be in the midst of nature and the magic of things.

In high summer as we first looked out onto the heath from the road we would be dazzled by the brilliant white of cotton-grass whose downy heads looked from a distance just like flowers. The presence of these grasses, which Jacob always explained to me were of no agricultural value and whose long silky hairs were too brittle to be made into thread of any kind, told us that if we got too close to them we were liable to get our feet wet.

Here where the cotton-grass grew, the flora of the heath merged into the bog, the wet acid peat and the sphagnum moss.

'Na then, lad, stand still, will yer, if tha wants to see summat.' Jacob's stern words would always bring my youthful and over-enthusiastic run forward to a halt. 'Jus car quiet for a minute an' lissen.'

Jacob had the true countryman's power of observation, and could always see before I could exactly where a hare had her form or a bird her nest. As we stood still among the grasses of the heath my mind would gradually start to become attuned to nature's music around me, the humming of bees, the clicking of grasshoppers and to the bird and insect life which lay at hand.

Here on the heath when I was with old Jacob I learnt my real lessons in 'nature study'. It is true that there was a short weekly lesson under that title at school but it generally seemed to consist of tuning into the schools broadcast on the wireless and listening to about twenty minutes of crackly, indecipherable birdsong. No birdsong hereabouts ever seemed indecipherable to old Jacob as quietly and patiently he sought to pass on his knowledge to me. As we stood and looked upwards beyond the heath to the heather moors, home of the red grouse, the snipe and the golden plover, I would become more and more aware of the many different birdsounds around me, the distant cooing of pigeons in the woods below, the persistent call of a faraway cuckoo and on the moors above, the wild weird cry of the curlew and the curious bleating sound of the snipe (which Jacob said was caused by the vibration of its wing and tail). Immediately above us the air would be full of the call of peewits and the glorious spirit-free sound of a multitude of skylarks.

'Time to move on lad', Jacob would say after a while.

We would then make our way through the cotton-grass and clouds of orange-brown small heath butterflies to an outcrop of huge stones at the far end of the heath known as 'the crag'. After we had climbed to the top, Jacob would sit down, light his pipe, look out over the heath and then start talking to me about his life and some of the characters he had known.

His tales and descriptions were peppered with lots of good well-used Yorkshire words and expressions like 'grand', 'champion', 'wick', 'reet', 'nowt o' t' soart', 'ovver theer', 'it is an' all' or 'it is that', 'nobbut just', 'off-comed un', 'appen', 'gormless', and my favourite of all, 'yonderly', to describe an old lady who lived in a dream world or who was, as we would say today, not all there. He would also use the expression 'Na then' in at least three different senses, as a greeting, as a warning, or as an expression of surprise.

I had wanted to learn about real Yorkshire words and speech ever since the day I had gone to my village playground as a very small boy and had been asked a question by a village lad which I totally misunderstood. I thought he had asked me if my name was Brian and I had politely replied that I was not called Brian but John. It turned out that the question he had actually been asking was 'Do yer want brayin?' Having misunderstood the question and having failed to 'leg it' quickly enough I found out immediately at first hand exactly what 'brayin' meant as I made it back home with a bloody nose and torn clothes.

It wasn't just entomology, botany and ornithology I learnt from old Jacob, it was etymology as well. He had the typical Yorkshire sense of humour and did a nice line in understatement which is perhaps the hallmark of the Tyke wit. After being snowed in with twenty foot drifts for a fortnight he would remark to anxious friends, 'T' weather's bin a bit old-fashioned'; and when he was very old and had gone with his 'missus' (as he always called her) to the funeral of one of his contemporaries he was heard to ask her afterwards, 'Well, lass, dus't tha reckon it's worth us goin' home for us tea?'

He was always philosophical about matters of life and death, and he delighted in pointing out to me his favourite inscription on one of the graves in the village churchyard: 'Farewell, earth, I've 'ad enough o' thee'. Although neither Jacob nor his missus were churchgoers they both possessed hearts of pure gold, always on the look out to help a neighbour, to visit someone in hospital or just to spend time with people who needed their comfort and support for whatever reason. Theirs was surely the best kind of charity, practical, unheralded and without boast. In Chaucer's words 'they used gladly to do wel'. Their philosophy was perhaps best summed up in a few lines they penned under their signatures in my autograph book:

'Count not your treasure in silver and gold

For these you will leave behind

But count it instead in the friends that you make

And the good you can do for mankind.'

For a boy to have such friends and mentors was fortunate indeed. Their philosophy and attitude to life served to reinforce what I was learning at home, particularly from my mother who was another who 'used gladly to do wel' and who was and still is the kindest, most considerate and most generous of women.

I still go back to the heath by the crag from time to time but it is not, I think, always wise to return to the favourite haunts of childhood. At any rate I'm glad old Jacob can't see it now for its very existence is threatened by the encroachment of a massive conifer plantation which each year is extended to take in a little more land so that steadily every year the heath diminishes in size.

I am prepared to concede that an individual conifer in the right place can be an attractive tree but to my mind the serried ranks of light-and-life destroying conifers so beloved of the Forestry Commission and commercial woodland owners are utterly alien to the English countryside and should have no place in it. I'm sure old Jacob would have had a choice Yorkshire word for them.

I reflect as I look out over this heathland which was so special to both of us that if the conifer growth remains unchecked, in a few short years it will have completely disappeared, along with the small heaths, the cotton-grass and the sphagnum moss. 'Does this matter?' I ask myself. After all there cannot be that many of us who care for such things and the majority of the general public probably won't even notice what is happening or realise that they are losing part of their natural heritage.

All I can honestly say is that it matters intensely to me, and whenever I sit on the crag looking out over the heath where old Jacob used to light his pipe and talk, philosophise and teach me all manner of things about nature and the countryside, I find myself instinctively repeating the lines of Gerard Manley Hopkins in his poem *Inversnaid*:

> 'What would the world be, once bereft
> Of wet and of wildness? Let them be left
> O let them be left, wildness and wet
> Long live the weeds and the wilderness yet.'

If the heath by the crag was our special place, it is with his beloved allotment that I shall forever associate old Jacob. Strange to say, it is in general most unusual for a farmer to like gardening but old Jacob's pride and joy was his allotment where he grew far and away the best soft fruit and finest vegetables in the village.

His soil was always deep black, loamy and as gardeners say 'friable'. His gardening was wholly intuitive. I doubt if he ever read a gardening book in his life. He always maintained that planting and growing were just common sense, and he was wont to quote the old saying: 'This rule of gardening ne'er forget, to sow dry and to set wet.' I once asked him to tell me the secret of his success, and he replied 'Its nowt really, just common sense and muckwatter'. Old Jacob was a muck-and-magic gardener alright - but the best I ever knew. He believed that in gardening as in life if a job was worth doing it was worth doing properly.

His allotment has long since been concreted over for housing development, but in my mind's eye I can still picture old Jacob standing there, wearing boots and a collar stud, puffing contentedly on his pipe, fondling his gleaming lovingly-cared-for silver spade while quietly saying to me about a neighbouring gardener, ' 'E's nobbut blackin' it ovver lad'. Everything old Jacob did was done conscientiously and painstakingly. Whatever the job - from winter digging to staking pea rods - he knew there was a right way and a wrong way to tackle it. From this most wonderful mentor I learnt, among many other things, two of the most important attributes of a legal practitioner - caution and care.

For some reason many people remember their Latin teacher and I am no exception. I was taught classics by a reverend gentleman named George Peachey, a High Tory, a pipe smoker and a brilliant scholar, who demanded nothing less than perfection from his pupils. He also taught me a lot about cricket, chess, amateur dramatics, religion, music, natural history and life. I recall that he was at his most unhappy if in the fifteen minute break between Latin lessons he had failed to complete *The Times* crossword puzzle. There was one occasion when he caught some of us smoking cigarettes and instead of beating us, the standard penalty for this offence in those days, he surprised us by gently admonishing us and advising us to take up a pipe.

'My boys', he said, puffing at his own favourite briar, 'a pipe will do you much less harm and it has the considerable advantage of keeping the end of your nose warm in winter.'

I would guess that my generation of schoolboys was about the last one to hear and occasionally understand jokes in Latin. Canon Peachey had a fondness for such jokes and quotations both in the pulpit and the classroom. Afterwards we would await his invariable dictum that he would under no circumstances translate them , except if there were ladies present. I doubt if he could get away with such discrimination these days!

One of his favourite stories concerned the visit of a stranger to an enclosed order of monks. It was a firm rule at this monastery that strict silence was to be observed during meals but that, in a case of emergency, speech was permitted, provided that it was in Latin. The calm silence of the evening meal was suddenly broken by the visitor speaking to his neighbour. There were frozen looks all round. He failed to take the hint and carried on talking - and talking what is more in English - whereupon the presiding abbot banged on the table, stood up, pointed his finger at the visitor and said 'Nunc, tunc' - which I suppose is the Latin equivalent of old Jacob's 'Na then'!

I was also taught at school by another parson, the Reverend Jim Murton, who was the complete opposite in every way to my classics master. His whole attitude to life had been conditioned by his experience as a curate in a rough area of Sheffield where he had encountered acute poverty and unemployment, and by a subsequent ministry in Egypt where he had seen dirt, squalor and disease. He was a socialist but there was no envy or vindictiveness in his socialism and he was one of the sincerest and most generous Christians I ever knew.

Partly as as result of these two parsons' influence, and partly because a lawyer above all others should be able to see things from every point of view, I have never been quite sure what my politics are. I have always believed in the British 'middle way', or what Horace called 'the golden mean'. I think that great writer, countryman and statesman John Buchan got it about right when he said:

'Thank God we shall always have both conservatives and radicals among us for they represent eternally the two sides of the human head. Both defend a truth which is not all the truth.'

There was a short time as a boy when I wanted to become involved in politics. I even contemplated trying to become prime minister. Fortunately for the country I decided to practise law instead.

An Articled Clerk I Soon Became

It is always said by Lancastrians that the only acceptable Yorkshireman is the one who has been educated in the red rose county. True or not, I will just have to live with the fact that I spent five years at a Lancashire public school:

> 'Where the stark north air
> Whirls round the Square
> At Rossall by the sea.'

When I eventually left school, without too much regret, at the age of eighteen I had gained a place to read law at Leeds University. At that time it was possible to combine taking a degree with the service of articles of clerkship. I knew that the degree course was likely to prove academic rather than practical in character, so it seemed sensible to get an idea of what sort of job I was likely to be doing once I had finished my three years.

I already knew where I wanted to practise, so the first task was to find a local solicitor brave enough to take me on. Secondly I had to persuade a committee of distinguished elder statesmen of the profession that I was a suitable person to be articled and thus obtain the Law Society's formal approval to my entry into the profession.

So it was that, shortly after starting my degree, I attended two interviews. The first was with my prospective principal, Phillip Lytton, senior partner in the old-established Denley firm of Boothroyd and Lytton. He struck me immediately as a most impressive lawyer, but I knew from his direct approach that serving my articles with him would be no picnic. Though, as I stood before him, he looked distinguished and rather severe, I could tell by the mischievous twinkle in his eyes that he had a sense of humour. I felt instinctively that there would be some lighthearted moments in amongst the hard work he obviously had in store for me.

'I believe in throwing articled clerks in at the deep end', he said bluntly, 'you can start with me as soon as you like.'

'Will you be preparing the deed of articles of clerkship for signature?', I asked somewhat naively.

'Certainly not!', he replied. 'You should draft your own articles and bring them to me for approval.'

Suitably chastened, I went to look up precedents for the drafting of my own deed of articles of clerkship. Modern day articled clerks would be amused by the final clause in the deed which stipulated that 'in consideration of my services' the solicitor would pay me the weekly sum of two pounds fifteen shillings. Actually, I thought I was fortunate. Some twenty-five years earlier my uncle had paid a firm of solicitors a premium of five hundred pounds for the privilege of being articled.

The first hurdle, that of finding articles, having been surmounted it now only remained for me to satisfy the Law Society interviewing committee that I was a person of suitable calibre to be admitted to articles.

When I attended this all-important interview I was ushered into a large room with an old-fashioned partners' desk standing in the middle of it. Sitting behind this desk were what looked like three solicitors who could have all come straight out of a Dickens novel. One had mutton chop whiskers, another was wearing a heavy gold watch chain and all three had a copy of *The Times* beside them.

On the whole I felt a little intimidated, but my nerves disappeared after the one with the mutton chop whiskers asked:

'Do you play cricket, Mr Francis?'

I suspect a 'no' at that point would have meant my looking for an alternative career. But when I told him I did they seemed satisfied, no doubt concluding that if I was a cricketer I must naturally follow the morals of the game which we had been taught at school - like playing with a straight bat, and all that.

So like most things in life you dread or worry about, the interview turned out to be far less painful than I had anticipated. On the whole the members of that committee seemed rather more interested in my family and my interests outside the law than in my reasons for wanting to enter that great profession. The unspoken question seemed to be 'Is he the right sort of chap?' Fortunately for me the committee gave their seal of approval and wished me luck in my legal career. I was now all set to take my first steps in my chosen profession.

If I had thought for a minute that serving articles of clerkship was going to be easy I was soon to be rudely awakened. Phillip Lytton had already told me at our first interview that he intended to throw me in at the deep end, not because he was an unkind man - far from it - but because he firmly believed that this was the quickest and best way to learn.

So it was that in my very first week of articles I appeared in chambers before a High Court judge on a bail application, served numerous writs and was rushed into a remote part of the dale to take a statement from a Mr Fred Holcross, who was a hundred years old, regarding a dispute over a right of way. If I had expected to find a centenarian who was confused, senile and housebound, I was about to be surprised. I was met at his cottage gate by a remarkably spritely looking old boy who was obviously expecting me.

'Na then, lad, do they call thee Perry Mason?'

'Well not exactly, sir' I replied. I thought I ought to make some small talk to break the ice, so rather shyly I said to him, 'I expect you've lived here long, Mr Holcross.'

'Aye lad, an' I 'aven't finished living 'ere yet', he replied sharply.

'Oh'. I paused. 'Well, I'd be grateful if you could tell me something about this right of way I wrote to you about.'

'Well, it were back in t' summer o' 1879 when there were a bit on a ruck 'tween my old gran'father Jimmy 'olcross and yon neighbour on 'is, Stan 'iggins - I'm not goin' too fast for thee, am I lad?'

I shook my head as I struggled to keep up with his lively patter. He then proceeded with absolute lucidity to give me a detailed history of the right of way stretching back the best part of his lifetime. His account would have been a credit to any lawyer.

' . . . well, t' job went quiet ivver after that, an' I can tell thee straight that t' reet o' way tha's on about 'as bin used by us 'olcrosses as well as yon 'igginses for all them years up to t' present time.'

That day I knew what it was to feel humble.

The next day I knew what it was like to feel ignorant. I was sent on what was called a 'taxation of costs' before the local county court registrar. It was a good job I had time to look it up, because before I did so I thought I was being expected to argue some matter with the Inland Revenue, whereas in fact I was concerned with an assessment of legal costs in a county court case. No wonder the great British public get confused about the law and its terminology, I thought.

Over the next months I learnt and learnt quickly. Phillip Lytton took great care to ensure that as a prospective solicitor in general practice I obtained a wide experience. It is quite astonishing how varied the work can be in small country practice. There were contracts and conveyances, wills and trusts, partnership agreements and company formations, divorce petitions, commercial and agricultural agreements and endless court forms of every conceivable variety. I reckoned that by the end of my articles I had at least touched upon every aspect of legal work, with the possible exception of marine insurance!

Articled clerks are also expected to make themselves useful around the office, and over the period of my articles I did nearly all the routine office jobs, though in some cases unbelievably badly. I filed, I copied plans, I wrote up the postages book, I put up shelves in the strongroom (which, to my partners' surprise, still stand to this day). I acted as receptionist, telephonist, book-keeper, cashier, and general factotum. I sometimes had to type my own letters, which is a very slow business when you can only use two fingers. An articled clerk is in a curious position, being neither one of the staff nor one of the bosses. You just have to adapt as best you can and play it all by ear.

I got through, thanks mainly, of course, to the efforts of my principal and his partners but also to the help and encouragement given to me by the staff.

The senior partner at Boothroyd and Lytton was Cyril Boothroyd, who was just about to retire when I joined the firm. Cyril was a gentleman solicitor of the old school, courteous, conscientious, painstaking and always concerned for the welfare of his clients. He never commenced an interview until he had first enquired at some length as to the health and well-being of the client and his family, and I have read letters written by him to clients after death or some other tragedy had struck which were couched in terms of the greatest possible kindness, sympathy and understanding.

Of course there were clients who took advantage of his kindness. He probably undercharged all of his practising life, and it was absolutely against his principles to send an 'account rendered' to a client, let alone sue him for payment of an unpaid bill.

Because he was a man of such uprightness and integrity he was occasionally the target of friendly leg-pulls by other professionals in Denley. On one occasion he wrote a letter in the most polite terms to a local firm of estate agents who were responsible for managing his office premises on behalf of Cyril's landlord. Cyril's complaint was that there was a leak in the gutter which was causing water to drip down onto his clients as they were entering the office. The senior partner of the estate agents wrote back to say that he was extremely sorry to hear that his clients were 'getting soaked', as he had always heard that Cyril's fees were most reasonable!

There was another time when a party of professional people from Denley, including Cyril, went for a night out to the City Varieties in Leeds. At the same performance there happened to be a party from Denley Working Men's Club. Now the same estate agent who had written to Cyril about his leaking gutter had a great reputation as a practical joker, and he decided that this was the occasion for another leg-pull at Cyril's expense. So he conspired with the master of ceremonies for the evening, and in the middle of the performance the MC came on stage to make an announcement:

'Ladies and gentlemen, I am very pleased this evening to welcome the large party from Denley, including their well-known local solicitor, Mr Cyril Boothroyd.'

As he laid a great theatrical emphasis on those last words, a huge spotlight swung across the theatre to pick out Cyril in the stalls. Immediately everyone from Denley broke into very loud and spontaneous applause. Poor Cyril, a shy, retiring man by nature, was absolutely mortified and wished only at that point that the floor should open and swallow him up. In retrospect, however, I doubt whether this little stunt at his expense did him any harm at all - in fact it probably did him quite a bit of good, because the party from the working men's club thereafter regarded him as 'one of the lads'.

The staff at Boothroyd and Lytton were presided over by the redoubtable Miss Beaumont whose countless years of service to the firm had made her a legendary fount of wisdom and knowledge, a role she still fulfilled until her recent retirement. Not only did she have an unrivalled experience of every aspect of office management and of the work of the practice, but she also possessed an encyclopaedic knowledge of all things pertaining to Denley, its people and our clients.

Superb typist, shorthand writer and drafter of documents though she certainly was, perhaps her greatest asset lay in her detailed knowledge of the clients, their families and their problems. I would mention that a particular client was coming to see me and she would say, 'Ah, yes, Mr Francis, I remember we acted for his father in 1947 in buying a plot of land between the old chapel and the Denley Building Society office and there was some trouble over a right of way.'

She was also the salvation of us all when it came to finding files or deeds which had been lost in the office. We would spend ages looking everywhere, and having exhausted all the impossible as well as the possible places we would turn to Miss Beaumont in despair. Within a few minutes she would invariably find the missing article. A friend to the partners and to the staff, she was the best guide to what goes on in a solicitor's office any articled clerk could possibly have had.

During my articles I learnt that a major part of legal practice is spent seeing clients. I saw my principal interviewing many clients and advising them on their problems with great skill and sympathy. I learnt from him the importance of conveying to the client the feeling that he or she is the most important person in the world and that, however big your case load, their case is the one you are concentrating on and the only one which matters. I discovered at a very early stage that the vast majority of clients are splendid and delightful people, but there is always a residue of difficult clients whose cases cause untold anxiety and trouble. Phillip Lytton always referred to such clients as 'MB's' - miserable fellows, or something like that.

Law Student

Whilst I was learning the practical side of law in Denley, I was trying to get to grips with academic law at Leeds University. Whilst my reading of Classics at school gave me some advantage when it came to Roman law, I must confess that now all I can remember of Roman law is that you could legally acquire a slave by announcing, to one and all as it were, 'I declare this man to be mine by Quiritary right'. I also vaguely remember that there were three ways of freeing a slave but in twenty-five years of practice in Denley I have not as yet been called upon to bring them to mind!

It is funny how often it's the small, offbeat and usually useless bits of information and knowledge that stay in the mind. I learnt that equity (like the British army) does not help volunteers, that gavelkind was a peculiar form of land tenure mainly restricted to Kent, and that there was a mediaeval form of conveyance known as 'feoffment with livery of seisin'.

In criminal law I was told that in Saxon times that there were three methods of trial: by witnesses (not unlike modern proceedings); by compurgation (in other words getting good witnesses for the reliability of your oath); and by ordeal, for example being thrown into a pond to see if you drowned, or if you were injured whether God healed your wound within a certain time. It was pretty rough justice in those days!

In jurisprudence I remember only Aquinas' concept of law that:

'Human law has the quality of law only insofaras it proceeds according to right reasoning, insofaras as it deviates from reason it has the quality not of justice but of violence.'

I recall that definition because I suppose it equates most closely to the average citizen's idea of British justice. It always comes to my mind whenever a client says, after losing a case he could not conceive of losing, 'Do you call this British justice, Mr Francis?' Solicitors constantly have to remind their clients that law and justice are by no means always the same thing.

For three years I was learning all the facets of our legal system, but perhaps more importantly I was seeing and learning something of life as well. The great thing about being a student is that you enjoy freedom without responsibility, time to think, talk and wonder without the cares of family and earning a living. Apart from our work - which none of us seemed to take too seriously - we laughed a lot, talked a lot, drank a lot and like every generation of students before us we were absolutely convinced that we knew all the answers to the world's problems. In retrospect I find myself mildly suprised that I ever got a degree at all, let alone with respectable honours.

So there I was learning the law by experience in the office and in theory at university. The two were so contrasting as to verge upon the absurd. I was learning how to free slaves in the morning and how to write up the postage book in the afternoon, at university how to interpret the United Nations Charter and at the office how to advise a Yorkshire farmer that he had no case (answer - very bluntly!).

When it came to giving blunt advice to farmers without causing offence, Phillip Lytton was a past master.

'Sometimes you've got to speak to clients in the only sort of language they understand', he would say to me.

I recall one particular farmer who, on being advised he had a case which was not worth pursuing, became very red-faced and banged his fist on my principal's desk.

'To 'ell wi' t' bloody law, it's not reet, it's a matter o' principle like an' I'll tek it to t' highest court in t' land.'

'Have you got your cheque book on you?', asked my principal.

'Aye, I 'ave as it 'appens. Why?'

'Because principles are fine as long as you realise they can sometimes cost money.

If you want me to go on with this case will you please write me out a cheque for one thousand pounds on account of costs.'

For the first time during the interview the client's resolve visibly faltered and his case came to an end right there.

There was something else I noticed about my principal. Not a man to waste time on small talk with clients, he liked to get down to brass tacks straight away. He could be very direct sometimes. His first words to a surveyor who had consulted him on a professional negligence case were 'Are you insured, Jack?'

A fair but very demanding taskmaster, he expected articled clerks to have done their homework. Woebetide me if I hadn't read a file properly before going to his office to discuss it with him. He didn't like sloppy work and still less did he like to be told that something he wanted to be done couldn't be done. On one occasion he had sent me to an out of town county court to issue a witness summons but the court rejected it.

'The wording is right but it's on the wrong form', I was told.

When I returned to Denley and reported my failure my principal was furious:

'Go back straight away and tell them that if the words are right they must issue it on lavatory paper if necessary.'

As I thought about this instruction on my journey back, it didn't seem wise for a callow youth to put it in quite those words to a chief clerk of over thirty years standing at the county court, but I managed to get it issued all the same in my own way and using my own words.

'Well, John', said Phillip Lytton at the end of my articles, 'I judge that you are now ready as you ever will be to be let loose on the great British public!'

All I had to do now was to pass the solicitors' qualifying exam.

The Solicitors' 'Final'

For aspiring solicitors of my generation, all roads led either to Lancaster Gate or to Guildford in Surrey. Here the College of Law ran crash courses preparatory to the taking of the solicitor's qualifying exam, or 'final' as it was known. It is a matter of surprise to some people that it is generally considered more difficult to qualify as a solicitor than as a barrister. Certainly law and accountancy are thought to be among the two most difficult professions in which to qualify and always seem to attract a high failure rate.

The six months I spent at Guildford were certainly a time of concentrated hard work but, as is invariably the case with any group of people thrown together in a common endeavour, there emerged a natural fellowship and camaraderie which helped everyone to persist. Rather like National Service, those who went through it enjoyed it rather more in recollection than they did at the time.

My time there was largely spent sweating away in a stuffy attic bedroom of the digs which I shared with two fellow law students. These digs were presided over by a splendid widow lady called Mrs Gillotson, known to generations of law students as 'Ma Gilly'.

Hers was an unenviable position because her duties were by no means limited to looking after her 'boys', as she always called us. Also living under the same roof were her friend and companion Emily, her daughter, her son-in-law and their four children, including a very lively and peace-shattering baby. Ma Gilly ruled over this varied household in a strict but kindly manner and was wonderfully tolerant of our occasional student excesses, including the time I was taught a particularly severe lesson by a local cider!

Ma Gilly expected her 'boys' to be punctual for meals, to eat everything laid before them, and of course to pass the final. She was fond of reminding us all that her previous boys had done so without exception. Failure on our part in any of these matters was something unheard of and not to be countenanced.

Being punctual for meals was not difficult but eating them was a different matter. We knew she would take it as a supreme personal insult if we did not finish the last crumbs of the huge pies and puddings which she laid before us at evening meal as her 'pièce de résistance' to a filling soup and a mammoth main course.

'Come on, you must eat, John, you really must eat. I've told you before, it's not on sale or return', she would say if I appeared to be struggling. 'You can't expect to pass the final if you don't eat properly.'

It's not surprising that after one of Ma Gilly's evening meals her charges felt obliged, if only for the sake of their digestive systems, to go out for at least an hour's walk as a prelude to further study, half an hour in the pub, a game of dominoes and bed.

As I observed my fellow students I often thought how much cleverer than I most of them seemed to be, and that perhaps I should be doing something else with my life. I had to keep reminding myself of the adage that the most brilliant lawyers do not usually make the best solicitors.

There were a few students (infuriatingly there always are) who seemed to sail through the course effortlessly and without any apparent application. They were the earnest young men who came into lectures carrying *The Times* under their arms and who asked erudite questions to which they already knew the answers. For the majority of us, however, it was quite simply a case of getting down to it and sweating it out.

If the other law students made me feel rather ignorant, the Guildford locals often made me feel like somebody from another planet. This was the 'gin and jaguar' country with which we northerners were totally unfamiliar. The locals weren't used to northern things, such as snow for instance. There was one day and one day only while I was there when it snowed. It hardly covered the ground and would not even have provoked comment in the Dales, but the locals, dressed to the eyeballs in thick coats, scarves and hats, looked on it as if it was the North Pole.

They were pleasant enough but their ignorance of, and prejudice against, the north of England took me by surprise. I had heard that this prejudice existed but did not really believe it until I experienced it. This was nearly a quarter of a century ago but it would not surprise me at all if there are still people in the south of England who picture the north as one vast industrial landscape full of factories, slag heaps, mill chimneys and terrace houses populated entirely by people who say 'Ea, ba gum' every second sentence. I strongly suspect that more missionaries are needed down there!

As the course went on, we all became more and more pessimistic as we began to appreciate the extent of our task. After the last test papers, the course management published their assessment of our individual chances of success. I seem to remember that mine was 'possible pass'. After the course came the exam itself - and what a stamina test that was. Seven three hour papers in three and a half days. During that particular week I probably knew more law than at any time in my practising life, most of which I have never had to use since.

After the exam, the agony of waiting, and after the waiting, the result - which by tradition is first made available to the finalists in the columns of *The Times*. On the day of publication I was at my newsagents at the crack of dawn where I discovered to my relief and delight that I had passed and would shortly be enrolled as a Solicitor of the Supreme Court. The weight of years of study was suddenly lifted from my shoulders, and in my naivety I genuinely thought that all my troubles were over. I had passed the 'final', qualified as a solicitor and seemed to be heading for a secure career. Little did I realise then that my problems hadn't even started.

My First Client

In the heady days after qualifying, when Phillip Lytton was kind - and brave - enough to offer me continued employment as an assistant solicitor, he clearly took a decision to lose no time in bringing me down to earth with a bump.

'Mr Francis will look after you very well, he's a very good young solicitor', said my employer, ushering a rather coarse and life-battered looking female client into my office.

Rather as one fears Greeks bearing gifts, solicitors learn to be on their guard when complimented by their principals or partners. Such flattery invariably means that the solicitor paying the compliment is anxious to divest himself of an awkward or unattractive client. All this, of course, I still had to learn.

After Phillip Lytton had beaten a somewhat hasty retreat, the woman sat down on the chair in front of my desk whilst holding a screaming child in her arms. For the next half hour - which seemed an eternity - I just could not get a single word in edgeways as, amidst the screams and tantrums of her child, the woman launched herself into a sustained and violent tirade against her husband.

' 'E nivver does owt in t' house, 'e gets proper drunk ivvery Friday an Saturday, 'e thumps me when 'e comes 'ome drunk an' wets t' bed. I've 'ad to burn two mattresses up t' now and as for 'im wi' other women, well luv, when 'e's bin out you should see 'is pants an t' lipstick on 'is shirt.'

And so she went on, and on, and on. I was about to try to tell her that I believed everything she said without the frightening prospect of having to inspect her husband's clothing when her ghastly child let out an almightly scream. Mum jumped up and a large pool of water was revealed on the chair which was slowly dripping onto the carpet.

'I'll 'ave to be off now, luv', she said. 'I'll be back another time to tell you it proper, like.'

I sighed to myself but she was gone before I could say a word. I was left in my office reflecting whether it was for this that I had spent all those weary hours sweating to become a solicitor. My thoughts were interrrupted by Phillip Lytton who poked his head round the door, surveyed my chair and the pool of water on top of it and smiled.

'Welcome to the practice of law', he said.

I had, I suppose, just been blooded.

Tales out of Court

Time Gentlemen Please

During the latter part of my articles I was given much more responsibility, to the extent that I was interviewing my own clients, drafting documents for them, handling their cases from start to finish and generally doing just about everything a qualified solicitor would do apart from representing them in court.

Now newly qualified solicitors are usually detailed to handle their firm's court work, and I was to be no exception. Advocacy is a part of legal practice which young solicitors learn by being thrown in at the deep end, by practice and by painful experience. It would perhaps surprise many members of the general public to know that the majority of solicitors don't do court work and never appear there during their careers. Maybe that's because most solicitors find other more profitable work to do - or maybe not enough of them have done amateur dramatics! Whatever the reason I think they all miss what should be an important part of every lawyer's experience in practice. At all events I was keen to have a go and I didn't have long to wait for my first court case.

'John, is your diary free next Friday?', asked Phillip Lytton, poking his head round my office door. 'There's a client here who needs representing in court. Over to you.' That was all he said.

Harry Atkins, the licensee of The Denley Heifer, came into my office with a very worried look on his face. He had been a conscientious and popular landlord in the town for many years, and now for the first time in his life he was in trouble with the police. He passed across my desk a summons for him to appear at Denley Magistrates Court to answer a charge that on a certain date 'he did knowingly sell intoxicating liquor to one Frank Leathley being a person under the age of eighteen years, namely fourteen years, contrary to section 169 of The Licensing Act 1964'.

'This isn't going to be an easy case to defend', I said with a touch of Yorkshire understatement. 'The key to it is whether you did knowingly serve an under-age person or - let me put it this way - whether you simply shut your eyes to the obvious. Now if you'd served a fourteen year old girl instead of a boy you might have stood a good chance. Magistrates know as well as anyone how difficult it is to tell the age of a teenage girl, particularly when she's not wearing a school uniform.'

'I know that, Mr Francis', replied my client, 'but you haven't seen Frank Leathley, have you?' I confessed that I hadn't.

'Well, he's over six feet tall, broad shoulders, the largest hands I've ever seen and looks like a Rugby League forward. I turn lots of under-age drinkers away but I really thought Frank was at least eighteen.'

'Alright', I said, 'we'll see what he looks like. But in the meantime can you find me a regular customer of yours who is definitely eighteen but looks about fourteen?'

He thought for a moment, then nodded and smiled.

The case duly came up for hearing before the Denley Magistrates, and my client pleaded not guilty to the charge against him. As the basic facts of the case were not in dispute, I didn't challenge the prosecution evidence that the police had found my client selling a pint of bitter in his pub to Frank Leathley, who on enquiry was found to be only fourteen years of age.

I limited my cross-examination to getting the officer in charge of the investigation to confirm that Harry Atkins was a man of unblemished reputation, well-respected in the town and with no previous convictions or record of any problems or disorder at his pub. I began the case for the defence by calling my client to the witness box and, after he had given the usual formal details of his name and address, I started my line of questioning.

'Are you the landlord of The Denley Heifer public house in Denley?'

'Yes.'

'How long have you been the landlord there?'

'Twenty years next month.'

'During that time have you ever had problems with under-age persons coming into your pub?'

'Yes, it's a difficult job these days telling who is over eighteen and who isn't.'

'What steps do you take to see that under-age persons are not served?'

'Well, I have a good look at everyone who comes into the pub and if I'm not sure about someone, then he or she doesn't get served. My staff are trained to do the same.'

'So it would be right to say that it is a problem of which you and your staff are well aware and that over the years you've refused to serve a number of young people?'

'Yes, and I'm afraid its a problem that's getting worse all the time.'

'Now, Mr Atkins, you've heard the police evidence about Frank Leathley. Do you accept that you served him with beer on the evening in question at a time when he was only fourteen years old?'

'Yes, Mr Francis, but I'd just never have believed he was only fourteen.'

During the prosecution evidence, Frank had been produced for the magistrates to see. There he stood at the back of the court, larger and even more mature looking than Harry had described to me. In fact, he looked almost as old as me! I continued my questioning.

'Had you ever seen Frank before the evening he came into your pub?'

'No.'

'Did you have any doubts about his age?'

'No, just looking at him I was quite sure he was over eighteen.'

Now, Mr Atkins, can you please tell the court whether there have been any occasions when you have turned away young people who have turned out to be eighteen?'

'Yes, several occasions.'

'Can you give a specific example?'

'Yes, there's a lad called David Horrox I refused to serve because he didn't look a day older than fifteen. He was very upset about it and came back the next day with this birth certificate which showed that the lad was telling the truth when he said he was over eighteen.'

I concluded the questioning of my client, and after he had been cross-examined by the prosecution I called David Horrox to give evidence. He confirmed as true everything my client had said about him in his pub, he had been back with his birth certificate the

next day and, yes, he was definitely over eighteen years old. He was not cross-examined.

At this point I asked the magistrates if Frank and David could both move forward and stand side by side immediately in front of the bench so that they could have a really good close look at them. So there the two lads stood, one a strapping twelve stone six footer who was fourteen years old and the other a five foot eight stone weed who was eighteen years old.

'You have now had the opportunity of seeing these two young men', I said to the magistrates at the end of my closing submission. 'Can you really be satisfied that my client shut his eyes to the obvious and that he knowingly served an under-age person?'

The magistrates must have put themselves in Harry Atkins' position because, after a very short retirement, they returned to announce that they found him not guilty.

As I enjoyed a celebratory pint afterwards with Harry at his pub, I was reflecting that I had been lucky with my first case. But as I started to appear in court on a regular basis I soon discovered that it is the cases you feel most confident about which should make you worry, and in which you are as likely as not to come unstuck.

Whether it was because of my unexpected success in the Harry Atkins case I do not know, but shortly afterwards I was appointed solicitor to the local Licensed Victuallers Association, which meant that I become increasingly involved in licensing cases. Every few weeks at Denley Court I was presenting applications to obtain official permission for drinking outside permitted hours in the form of 'an extension of hours' or 'an occasional licence'. The trick was to dress up an application for extra drinking time with a description likely to satisfy the licensing magistrates and come within their concept of 'a special occasion'.

What is a special occasion? Well, eighteenth and twenty-first birthday parties qualify and so, apparently, does an engagement party or a fishing match, but nineteenth or twentieth birthday parties won't do and neither will a stag night. With the recent relaxation of the licensing laws it has been made much easier to enjoy a drink at most sensible times of the day, but extensions sometimes still have to be sought.

Going into court on a regular basis meant that I spent a good deal of time listening to cases in which I was not involved. I learnt quite a lot as a result and I also got the occasional laugh. Magistrates courts are generally rather serious and businesslike places, but now and again something can happen in court to lighten this atmosphere.

Soon after starting my career as an advocate, I travelled to a rather remote court some distance from Denley to represent a valued client on a run-of-the-mill motoring offence. It is the custom in most courts to deal with the licensing applications first and then proceed with the rest of the court list. On this occasion, however, there was a juvenile case to be heard, and as often happened in a small country court in those days, the magistrates who sat in the licensing court also comprised the juvenile bench. The juvenile in question was charged with drinking in a pub whilst under age. There was no defence to the charge to which he pleaded guilty and was duly fined.

The same magistrates then proceeded to hear the licensing applications, and the very first on the list was by a local licensee for an extension of hours for an eighteenth birthday party. It then became apparent that the birthday boy in whose honour an extension of hours was being sought was the self-same boy who minutes earlier had pleaded guilty to under-age drinking! The dignity of the court was immediately disturbed by spontaneous laughter from everyone present, and even the chairman of the bench was seen to smile before he granted the application without further comment.

When Your Luck Doesn't Last

As I started to do more court cases I couldn't help noticing that the same names kept appearing at regular intervals on the court list. I suppose it's an ill wind that blows nobody any good, and it occurred to me that if I could acquire some of these persistent offenders as clients then I would have the chance of some repeat business!

There's a well-known story which solicitors tell against themselves of the man who walked into a solicitor's office and asked to be represented by him on a criminal charge. On going into his prospective client's background, the solicitor discovered that he had been represented previously on five occasions by another solicitor who had got him off each time.

'I can't understand why you've decided to change your solicitor', the solicitor said, 'when your previous solicitor has done so well for you.'

'I know that', said the client, 'but I didn't think his luck could last.'

I was reminded of this story when I represented a lorry driver called Billy Park several times during my first couple of years in the magistrates court. Now Billy was a damn good worker but his driving record was appalling. In the ten years since he first held a licence he had made no less than twenty-five court appearances for virtually every road traffic offence in the book from speeding to failing to keep proper records of his hours.

Without a driving licence he would have been unemployed, so it was essential that I should do everything possible to try to persuade the magistrates not to disqualify him. Because of previous endorsements on his licence, the magistrates were bound to disqualify him unless they found special reasons or mitigating grounds.

On each of the four previous occasions I had represented him at different magistrates courts, my main tactic had therefore been to call as a witness Billy's employer, a down-to-earth Yorkshire type by the name of Jake Arkwright. As he stood in the witness box facing the magistrates, Jake, with his rugged features, horny hands and hairy chest beneath an open-necked shirt, looked every inch a 'workers' boss' - the sort of employer who wouldn't ask his men to do anything he didn't do himself.

'Is your name Jake Arkwright and are you the proprietor of Arkwright Haulage?', I would ask him.

'Aye, t' business 'as bin mine sin' me father died ovver seven year ago', he would reply.

'Is the defendant Billy Park employed by your firm?'

'Aye, 'e is that an' 'e's bin wi' us for t' past five year.'

'What's his job with the firm?'

'Billy's one o' t' drivers, an' e' goes all ovver t' country wi' t' wagons for us.'

'I suppose he clocks up a big mileage over the course of a year?'

'Aye, 'e does a fair few mile does Billy. 'E's dead keen an' all an' a reet good timekeeper.'

I would then bring Jake to the crux of the matter.

'If Mr Park was to be disqualified from driving today, would you be able to keep him employed by your firm?'

'Nay, Mr Francis, not wi' t' best will in t'world. Billy's a driver, 'e can't do owt else an' if 'e can't drive e'll 'ave to go, like.'

My final question would always be:

'Mr Arkwright, would you please tell the court what you think of Billy as a worker?'

Jake would invariably reply:

' 'E's one o' t' best we've ivver 'ad, yer worship, we can't get lads like 'im round 'ere.'

Impressed by Jake taking the time and trouble to come to court and by his forthright evidence on behalf of 'one o' t' best he'd ivver 'ad', the magistrates decided not to disqualify Billy on all four previous occasions.

However the fifth time, Billy appeared at a court where this tactic had been used successfully before, and by ill chance the presiding magistrate had been sitting on the previous occasion. I didn't appreciate this at the time, so I went ahead and presented my case using the same tactics which had worked so well before. I put Jake through what was now his customary question and answer routine but as he concluded his evidence with the words 'E's one o' t' best we've ivver 'ad, we can't get lads like 'im round 'ere', I thought I detected a flicker of a smile on the face of the chairman of the bench. Unfortunately for Billy the chairman turned out to have a good memory, and after listening to the evidence he consulted his colleagues briefly and addressed himself to me:

'Mr Francis, I see that on no less than four previous occasions your client has not been disqualified - despite his shocking driving record. No doubt this has to some extent been because of the way his employer has given evidence in court. He has given evidence again today and it sounded very similar to what he said the last time he came before this court. I suggest that you consider varying your courtroom tactics next time, Mr Francis. And Mr Arkwright, I thank you for coming yet again to vouch for your employee, but I hope for your business's sake that you can get 'lads like 'im round 'ere'. Mr Park, you will be disqualified from holding or obtaining a driving licence for a period of six months.'

Billy's luck had finally run out . . . and so had mine.

The Case of the Precocious Redshank

By now I was starting to get to grips with the routine of magistrates court work and I was finding this to be as varied as the rest of my office work. It wasn't just licensing and road traffic cases I was handling - I was also representing clients on all manner of criminal charges, ranging from assault to burglary, from arson to disorderly behaviour and just about every kind of petty and sometimes not so petty crime committed in and around Denley.

In the vast majority of cases I was acting as solicitor for the defendant, but in a small number of cases I was also gaining experience as a prosecuting solicitor. I welcomed these opportunities, if only on the basis that it couldn't be a bad thing to see a case from the other side of the solicitors' bench for a change.

In fact I hadn't been doing court work for very long when I was instructed to conduct a private prosecution for alleged poaching against a young man by the name of Kevin Smith. My instructions came from a family friend, one Captain Jeremy Sproat, who owned a small country estate in the Vale of York. For some time past he had been having continual problems with young lads coming out from towns and cities, trespassing on his land, taking pheasants and hares and generally disturbing the game on his estate. At last his keeper had caught one of these poachers with a freshly-killed hare in his car and Captain Sproat was determined to use this opportunity to prosecute and get a conviction in the hope that Kevin and his kind would be deterred.

On the day in question the keeper had seen Kevin park his car at the side of the road, walk on to the captain's land and release a greyhound. He had continued to watch as Kevin worked over a ploughed field with his dog, then a meadow and a field of winter wheat, and as he was waiting he had seen the dog catch a hare and kill it. He had observed Kevin taking the hare back to his car, and it was there that he had finally caught up with him and confronted him. To the keeper's amazement, Kevin denied poaching, claiming that he had caught the hare on common land some distance away and had stopped his car and gone on to the captain's land to look for a redshank's nest as he was a keen birdwatcher. Taken aback by such a brazen attitude and bare-faced lie, the keeper was left completely speechless.

This was when my lifelong love of nature became of practical use, and I blessed the memory of old Jacob for what he had taught me all those years previously. I knew that in this part of the world, redshanks, which migrate in the winter to Africa and southern Asia, do not start nesting until the middle of April at the earliest. I supplemented my own knowledge of the bird with some careful reading and study of its nesting habits, and when I took the keeper's statement I found out that he knew quite a lot about the species too.

Normally when I go into court I take with me worthy and well-established law books such as *Stones Justices' Manual, Archbold on Evidence* or *Halsbury's Laws and Statutes*, but for this particular trial I went into court armed only with my *Hollom's Popular Handbook of British Birds*. All in all I felt I would be well prepared for the defence which I knew would he put forward in court.

The day of the trial came, and Kevin gave the same explanation to the court as he had when confronted by the gamekeeper. I felt an unusual sense of anticipation, for this was one cross-examination I was looking forward to conducting. After a few preliminary questions I felt I was getting into my stride.

'You admit that on the third of March you were trespassing on my client's land?', I asked.

'Aye, but I weren't doin owt wrong theer' replied Kevin.

'What were you doing there?'

'I were lookin' for a redshank's nest. I told t' keeper that at t'time.'

'You're a birdwatcher, are you?'

'That's reet, I spends me spare time in t' country looking at t' birds.'

'Do you normally take your greyhound with you on these expeditions?'

'Aye, what's wrong wi' that?'

At this stage Kevin seemed confident and I felt I was succeeding in lulling him into a false sense of security.

'You know a bit about redshanks, do you?' I continued.

'A fair bit', replied Kevin, 'I'm always on t' look out for 'em.'

'Well let's see what you can tell the court about redshanks. Where do they normally breed?'

'In t' fields like, cos they feed on corn.'

This was Kevin's first mistake and his confident smile started to disappear as I produced *Hollom's Popular Handbook of British Birds*, which until then I had concealed from his view.

'Would you accept from me and from this book that redshanks normally breed in marshes, don't feed on corn but eat insects, worms, shrimps and small frogs?'

'So, I were wrong about that', he replied sullenly.

'How many eggs are there normally in a redshank's nest?'

'Three', he replied. I knew he was guessing now.

'What colour are they?'

'Blue', came back Kevin. I produced the book again.

'Would you accept from me that there are normally between four and eight eggs and their colour is buff or greenish but definitely not blue?'

'If t' book says so', replied Kevin.

I judged the time had now come to move in for the kill.

'Would you mind telling the court, in your expert opinion, when does a redshank normally start nesting?'

There was a long silence. Kevin happened to glance up at the large clock on the courtroom wall, which had the inscription 'Tempus Fugit' underneath it. Unfortunately, one of the magistrates noticed Kevin's action and said to him:

'Yes, Mr Smith, I'm looking at the clock too, and if I may say so it is going a good deal faster than you are.'

I repeated the question to Kevin.

'In t' spring', he replied.

'Mr Smith, you say you were looking for a redshank's nest on the third of March' - and here I produced my book again - 'yet every bird book will tell you that redshanks do not normally start nesting until April at the earliest. For your story to be true, it would have had to have been a very precocious redshank in a forward season wouldn't it?'

Kevin's silence was broken by laughter around the court.

'You've been telling the court a fairy story haven't you? The truth is that you were poaching, weren't you?'

This moment was to prove the nearest I would ever get in years of court work to one of those American court room scenes epitomised in *Perry Mason* where a witness breaks down in tears and makes a dramatic admission of guilt.

Kevin didn't actually admit to poaching, but he didn't answer my last question either. At all events the case didn't last very much longer and he was duly convicted and heavily fined.

'Well, John', said Captain Sproat afterwards, 'I hope these lads from the city will go somewhere else now.'

It has been said that the average countryman ought to know and be able to recognise a minimum of thirty different kinds of bird. After this case the redshank certainly featured in my top thirty, but maybe a country solicitor should be able to do better than that, particularly if he conducts cases involving game birds and poaching!

The Spanish 'Interpreter'

I had been lucky in the redshank case. I knew exactly what my witnesses were going to say and I had a pretty good idea of what Kevin Smith was going to say, so I was able to prepare accordingly.

It remains true, however, that the unknown quantity in any court case is how well or how badly a witness will give evidence. Sometimes a witness will be so nervous and unforthcoming that every bit of evidence has to be dragged from him, other witnesses are so confident that they often ruin their own case by 'over-egging the pudding', but the worse kind of witness is the one who quite simply fails to 'come up to proof', as lawyers say. In other words the witness tells a totally different story in court to the one he has given to his solicitor before the case.

However, the greatest difficulty is probably presented by a witness who has a speech disability or who simply cannot speak English. In my early days of doing court work I had experience of both of these difficulties.

In one case I was instructed by a client who was deaf and dumb to file a petition for divorce against his wife on the grounds of her cruelty, and in court I was obliged to present his case with the assistance of a sign-language interpreter. There were about twenty other divorces listed for hearing that morning, but it was agreed that because of my client's special difficulties his case should be taken first.

I explained the position to the judge and told him that my client was particularly anxious that he should be treated just like everyone else. Like all the others that morning, his case was undefended. Undefended divorces in those days took about ten minutes on average, but by the time I had, via the sign-language interpreter, taken my client through all seventeen instances of his wife's cruelty set out in the petition, his case took the best part of an hour.

Judges are not in my experience as patient or considerate as they should be, but in this case the concern shown by this particular judge to a divorce petitioner with such a severe disability was exemplary.

Just as difficult for a defending solicitor is the case where his client does not speak or understand English. Manuel Gonzalez was a Spanish waiter who asked me to defend him on a charge of stealing a coffee pot from the Royal Hotel where he had been employed. The coffee pot, which had 'Royal Hotel, Denley' stamped upon it, had been recovered by the police from a display cabinet in his lodgings, which had been used by waiters from the hotel for several years.

Manuel's defence was that the coffee pot had already been in the display cabinet when he took up occupation and must therefore have been 'acquired' by the previous occupant. As my client did not read or understand English very well at all he had not realised it had belonged to the hotel where he worked!

The general public always find this hard to understand, but the plain truth always has been that it is no part of a defending solicitor's duty to make a judgement upon his client's guilt or innocence, but simply to put his client's case before the court to the best of his skill and ability.

In this case, however, I was privately inclined to believe in my client's innocence, as I felt it unlikely in the extreme that a thief would place a stolen coffee pot in a display cabinet positioned just inside his front door which would be seen immediately by anyone entering his house! I think in the end it was this point above all the others I made during the case which probably weighed most with the magistrates.

Even though Manuel had to give evidence through an interpreter, he made a very shrewd choice because as the case progressed his interpreter became so excited and emotionally involved on behalf of his fellow countryman that it became increasingly difficult to tell whether he was strictly confining himself to acting as an interpreter or whether he was giving evidence himself!

Without any doubt my little Spanish waiter was a forerunner of the waiter by the same christian name immortalised by Andrew Sachs in the TV series *Fawlty Towers*. Regardless of the question I put to him, the same answer came back via his interpreter.

'Mr Gonzalez, will you tell the court how long you have been employed as a waiter at the Royal Hotel, Denley.'

Manuel exchanged brief and excited words with his interpreter, who relayed his answer:

'Senor, he say he no taka coffee pot.'

'Can I put the question again. How long have you worked at the Royal Hotel?'

'He say he never taka nothing in his lifa.'

I looked at the magistrates and tried another question.

'Mr Gonzalez, can you explain why a coffee pot stamped 'Royal Hotel, Denley' was found in your lodgings?'

'Manuel tell me he never taka nothing in his lifa. He come from a good family, senor. He say he no taka coffee pot.'

I tried a number of different questions, but each got the same response, only with more and more emotion each time. Eventually the interpreter's excitement reached fever pitch and, gesticulating wildly, he exclaimed:

'Manuel say again he no taka potty coff, senor.'

I strongly suspected that this classic spoonerism came from the interpreter rather than from Manuel, but at all events it served to break the heightened tension as laughter rang round the court. At this point the chairman of the magistrates decided to intervene.

'I think we've got the gist of your client's evidence, Mr Francis', he said, allowing himself to smile slightly.

After I had made my closing submission, the magistrates retired for only a short time before returning. When the chairman announced a not guilty decision there was absolute pandemonium in the court for several minutes. Sitting at the back of the courtroom during the trial had been what looked like Manuel's entire family, together with a number of his compatriots. Upon hearing the verdict they broke into loud and spontaneous applause, clapping, singing and throwing their hats into the air as they rushed forward to mob him and congratulate him.

Before being lost in the crowd, Manuel just had time to bow to the chairman of the bench and exclaim 'Muchas gratias, senor, muchas gratias' before breaking down, weeping uncontrollably, and being borne in triumph from the court on the shoulders of his fellow countrymen like a victorious matador.

As I left the court surrounded by a crowd of excited and grateful Spaniards, I just managed to say thank you to Manuel's interpreter for his brilliant performance. There was no doubt that as an advocate, interpreter and witness combined he had been the star of the show. I had simply been a member of his cast.

'You Come Quick, We Got Plenty Trouble'

Bridge players always say that it is the next hand which matters not the last, and the same principle surely applies to court work. In any event you never have the time to glory in your triumphs or to reflect on what you should have said in the cases you lose. Perhaps it is just as well.

At any rate I found that the drama of Manuel's case was soon forgotten as I fell back quickly into the routine of my bread-and-butter cases in Denley - breaches of the peace, assaults, drunkenness, criminal damage and the like. There always seemed to be a steady flow of cases in which I represented youths charged with threatening and violent behaviour in and around Denley. In many of these cases it was the same youths whom I was representing over and over again. Many of these charges attracted guilty pleas and speeches in mitigation, but those which were contested usually meant making a wholesale attack upon the version of events given by the complainant or the police.

The two favourite places in the locality for trouble always seemed to be the bus station and the Chinese restaurant. For the most part the cases proved routine and unmemorable, but there was one which stood out. The case concerned two local lads, Pete and Dave, who had been charged under the Public Order Act with conduct likely to cause a breach of the peace in the local Chinese restaurant, which at that time was owned by a splendid if rather excitable Chinese gentleman known as Hubert Wong.

I was instructed to represent Pete, but Dave's parents didn't think a Denley solicitor was good enough for their son and arranged for him to be represented by one of the bigger city firms. However the partner whom they had instructed did not consider it worth his time and trouble to deal personally with what he regarded as a minor case 'out in the sticks' at Denley, and passed the file to his most junior assistant solicitor who had only just qualified. Unbeknown to Dave and his parents that young man had yet to make his debut at court. It was to prove a rough baptism.

The day of the trial duly came and both Pete and Dave pleaded not guilty when the charge was put to them. The prosecution case was that the two had entered the restaurant at about 10.30 pm one Friday evening after the pubs had closed and that they were both in an argumentative and aggressive mood. Mr Wong gave evidence that the two defendants had ordered a meal and had then proceeded to fool about, giving a mock demonstration of how to eat with chopsticks and deliberately spilling bamboo shoots, noodles and sweet and sour pork on the floor. According to the proprietor, both lads had gone on from there to complain about the food, use obscene language and generally disturb the other customers.

Finally, Mr Wong said, they had become increasingly aggressive and initially refused to pay the bill, whereupon he had called the police who had arrived in force and arrested them. Now all this evidence had been given in a hesitant manner and in broken English, so it was clear that his understanding of the language was limited to say the least.

I began my cross-examination of the proprietor by asking him if he often had to telephone the police to come to his restaurant. He agreed this was the case. I pressed the point further.

'Is it not a fact that you always telephone the police if you think there is the slightest chance of trouble?'

'Yes, sir, we call police if trouble', he replied.

'Do you agree that my client and his friend had finished their meal and paid the bill before the police arrived?'

'Yes, sir, they pay me before police come.'

'Were they not leaving your restaurant peacefully when the police arrived?'

This last question of mine was the crucial one, and when the proprietor appeared to nod his head in agreement I decided that was the moment for me to sit down. It was now the turn of Dave's solicitor to cross-examine Mr Wong. It would have been better if he had not done so.

'Mr Wong, are you telling the court that these two young men were leaving the restaurant peacefully when the police arrived?'

It now became only too apparent that Mr Wong had not properly understood my original question to him, for he now became very excited and animated.

'No, no, sir, you wrong, they make plenty trouble when police come, they not leaving when police come.'

My young friend from the city had just, to the very first question of the very first cross-examination he had conducted, been given a reply which he was not expecting. It is a situation which every defending solicitor has to face from time to time and it is one where a bit of acting experience comes in handy. On receiving a devastating reply to his question, the thespian solicitor's face will be a picture, not of unease or embarrassment, but of complete and utter incredulity that such a statement could be made in the serious expectation that it will be believed by the court!

As it was Dave's solicitor stood there silently for what seemed an eternity, unsure of how to react and obviously totally thrown out of his stride.

'Oh', he said, 'oh dear', and sat down.

After that it was clear that the two lads' defence - which had never really looked very promising anyway - was positively doomed. All I could do was to engage in what would in modern jargon be described as a 'damage limitation exercise' by trying to establish that the affair had been blown up out of all proportion. So I asked the principal police witness whether he had received many calls before from Mr Wong and he confirmed that this was the case.

'Did he always use words like 'you come quick, we got plenty trouble'?'

'Yes, something like that, sir', he replied.

In the end the magistrates were unsurprisingly not persuaded by my submission that Mr Wong clearly called the police whenever there was the slightest whiff of trouble, that there was no serious trouble in this case and the lads should be believed when they said they were peacefully leaving the restaurant when the police arrived. Pete and Dave were both duly convicted and fined, but did not seem too disturbed at the outcome.

'Well, you win some, you lose some', I reflected as I walked back to the office.

What Price a Reference

If breaches of the peace in and around Denley were a regular feature of my magistrates court practice, then the other very regular business in court lay in defending clients charged with motoring offences of one kind or another.

The most important of these cases were those where my client's driving licence was at stake. At one time my firm acted for a company which employed a large number of executives and sales reps. The possession of a driving licence by these employees was obviously a matter of fundamental importance. In the case of the sales reps in particular their annual mileage was greater than that of the average motorist so by the law of statistics alone they were more likely to fall foul of the road traffic statutes and regulations.

I was most frequently asked to represent them when they were at risk under the old 'totting-up' procedure, when they were likely to be disqualified for having three endorsements within three years. In those circumstances their endorsements were totted up and disqualification followed - unless the court could be persuaded either that there were special reasons for not endorsing or mitigating grounds for not disqualifying.

My tactic in such cases was to try to persuade magistrates that the possession of a driving licence was essential for the job, and that unemployment and hardship would result from a driving ban. In support of such a submission it was always my practice wherever possible to call one of the senior management as a witness to testify as to the excellent character of the rep in question and to confirm that a driving ban would result in the loss of his job. Whilst such a reference can always be given in writing, it has always

been my belief that the evidence is much more likely to impress the magistrates if given in person. This was, after all, a tactic which I had used successfully with Billy Park more than once - until I came unstuck.

There was one occasion when I attended an out of town magistrates court to represent a sales rep in one of these typical totting-up cases. When I arrived I found that there were four local solicitors who also had totting-up cases. They were all courteous enough to suggest that, since I had come from out of town, my case should be heard first. Having employed my usual tactic of calling my client's managing director to give evidence on his behalf, I ended my submission thus:

'Whilst your worships are well aware that a written reference can be given very easily and may not be worth very much, when an employer is prepared to give up time to attend court on behalf of his employee then that should carry very much greater weight.'

The magistrates were duly impressed and found grounds for not disqualifying my client.

I turned round to leave the court, only to see the four local solicitors all looking daggers at me. They were each holding written references in their hands!

'Make Your Bill a Big One'

The client ushered into my office by my receptionist was one I could not recall seeing before. He introduced himself to me as Harry Jenkins, a sales rep, and showed me a summons for him to appear at Denley Magistrates Court for an alleged drink driving offence. I had not acted for him before, but he explained to me that he had appeared at magistrates courts over the years in different parts of the country, invariably for different kinds of road traffic offences. He then went on, as if to flatter me:

'I always try to instruct the solicitor who is best known in his local court.'

This seemed to me to be good thinking. I have always felt that a reasonably competent local solicitor is likely to obtain better results than a flash city solicitor who is brought in for a case. Local magistrates tend to regard such 'outsiders' with a degree of suspicion.

At all events, Harry's flattery worked and I agreed to represent him. Whether it was his flattery, his smooth sales rep patter, or a combination of the two I am not sure, but there was something about him which didn't seem quite right. I had at the back of my mind the old nursery rhyme:

'I do not like thee Dr Fell, the reason why I cannot tell.'

The case was obviously of great importance to Harry, as a conviction would have resulted in a mandatory driving disqualification which would in turn have meant the loss of his job. In the event I managed to obtain an acquittal following my technical legal submission that on the evidence the prosecution had failed to prove that he had been driving or attempting to drive within the meaning of the law at the relevant time.

I came out of the court feeling rather pleased at the outcome of the case. It had after all involved a lengthy and careful consideration of the law and some burning of the midnight oil the previous night to prepare my submission. But if I was pleased, my client was overjoyed.

'Thank you, Mr Francis', he said as he shook my hand vigorously. 'You've saved my job.' And then he added, 'You'll make your bill a big one, won't you?'

I should have known then, I suppose, but in my moment of glory I thought little of it. 'Right you are', I said. We shook hands and left the court.

I sent my bill. I sent a second bill, and a third. Finally I sent him a letter threatening to sue him. The letter was only returned by the Post Office marked 'gone away'. There was absolutely no means of tracing him and I had no alternative but to write off the debt and put the case down to experience. It was at this point that I remembered again the words of the old nursery rhyme and added a few choice ones of my own!

A Fair Do

'T' trouble all started, your worships, when t' cat peed on t' mat.'

These were the unforgettable words used by a local solicitor to open a case in a domestic court in prewar Denley. As a young advocate I spent a good deal of time in the domestic court, usually asking the magistrates to make maintenance orders in favour of deserted and ill-treated wives.

There seemed to be an incredible number of such cases for a town as small as Denley. Bastardy or affiliation proceedings in respect of illegitimate children were not uncommon, and at that time there was still an aura of guilt and embarrassment surrounding such cases. Frequently the alleged father would admit paternity and, in these cases, orders would be made by consent without any difficulty, often the only argument being as to the amount of the child's maintenance. If paternity was denied the defence almost invariably was that the complainant had had sexual intercourse with one or more other men about the time of conception and so paternity could not be conclusively proved.

There was one memorable case that is so much part of local folklore as to be almost certainly apocryphal. There was a certain young woman who travelled from her village every Saturday night to the weekly dance in Denley. She was driven to the dance in a car which - apart from herself and the young man who drove - carried three other young men from the same village.

She must have been a lusty country girl, for the routine invariably was for her to have sexual intercourse with two of the young men on the way to the dance and with the other two on the way home. She soon became pregnant, gave birth to a child and applied to her local magistrates court for an affiliation order against one of the young men. When the case came on for hearing, he denied paternity and called his three friends to describe their Saturday evening 'routine' and to say that they too had had sexual intercourse with her and could each have been the father.

The magistrates retired for longer than usual and when they came back the chairman, a typically blunt Yorkshireman, addressed all four young men.

'Na then, lads you've had your bit of fun and now you're all going to pay for it. I could give you all sum advice but I doubt if tha's t' wit to tek it. The order of the court is that you will each pay seven shillings and sixpence every week for the child's maintenance.'

There was a shocked silence in court. The lawyers were all aghast. All four lads were, not surprisingly, advised that the order could not possibly be sustained in law, since as there could only be one father only one of them could in law be made to pay; an appeal was bound to be successful and should be pursued immediately.

However, the four lads would have none of it. They put their heads together briefly and then said with one voice.

'Nay, we're not going to appeal. We reckon it's a fair do.'

One of Those Days

It has always been my policy when going to court to make sure that I arrive early. That way I have found myself better prepared for my cases both mentally and physically. More important from a practical point of view, there is a better chance of having a quick word with the justices' clerk and getting my case on first.

One day I had arrived at an out-of-town court in plenty of time and I thought I would have a cup of coffee in the cafe which stood at the end of the car park. As I was walking across the car park towards the cafe, a large coach arrived containing a party of women who were obviously on an outing. To my consternation I noticed that the ladies were making for the same cafe but, having been brought up to be polite, I held back and allowed them all to go in front of me. When they had all been served and it was my turn at last I ordered my cup of coffee.

'How much do I owe you?' I asked the lady at the counter.

'You don't owe me anything,' she replied.

I was puzzled, and asked the question again.

'It's alright, luv, we never charge the driver.'

It was obviously going to be one of those days. Sure enough, by the time I got to court all the other solicitors had beaten me to it, had spoken to the clerk and got their cases on first. I took my seat and waited. The clerk addressed himself to the first defendant in the dock.

'What is your full name?'

'Freddy Fox,' came the reply.

'What is your occupation?'

'Chicken catcher,' said the defendant gravely.

It was quite a time before the defendant was able to satisfy the court that he was telling the truth and calm was restored.

When the laughter had subsided and Mr Fox's case had been dealt with, I was wondering how best to follow him when another solicitor asked if he could go before me in order to apply for an adjournment as his client had been admitted to hospital. The chairman of the bench conferred with his colleagues for a few minutes and then turned to the solicitor.

'Your client faces a very serious charge of handling stolen goods, and before we agree to your application for an adjournment we would like some more information. We are sorry to hear about your client but could you tell us please exactly why he has been admitted to hospital?'

The solicitor looked rather embarrassed, shuffling from one foot to the other.

'Well, your worship, I'm not sure how to put this but the fact is that . . .' - he paused - '. . . he fell off the back of a lorry.'

By this time I was regretting my pre-court coffee and wondering how on earth I was going to follow the two previous cases.

Poetic Justice

In terms of court work it was to be the magistrates court which was to be my main love and enduring preoccupation, and for the next fifteen years or so I was to spend at least one day a week representing clients at Denley Magistrates Court.

Although some cases were not guilty pleas, contested cases were the exception rather than the rule and much of my time was spent in preparing and putting forward pleas in mitigation. The most important and effective characteristic of a plea in mitigation, in my view, is sincerity. Those advocates who always try to portray their clients as angels and give totally false assessments of their behaviour and prospects for reform in fact do their clients a disservice in the eyes of the court.

Over the years any magistrate must hear the same familiar excuses from defending solicitors many, many times. There are a number of expressions repeatedly used by defending advocates which have become the clichés of the trade. Magistrates listening attentively to solicitors summing up must become tired of hearing the old phrases: 'he did it on the spur of the moment', 'he was short of money at the time', 'he came from an unhappy home', 'he had too much to drink' (surely an aggravating rather than mitigating circumstance), 'it was wholly out of character', and, worst of all, 'he now stands at the crossroads of life'.

It is, of course, the defending solicitor's duty to put before the court every conceivable and relevant mitigating factor, but the effectiveness of the mitigation is likely to be determined not by the repetition of standard clichés, but in thorough research into the client's background, the circumstances of the offence and putting forward realistic suggestions as to sentence. For my part I have always conscientiously striven to avoid the use of clichés in mitigation, and have possibly been one of the last solicitor advocates to quote Shakespeare, the Bible, Dickens and Latin on a regular basis. The important thing is to capture the attention of the court and then hold it.

Over the years I have tried with mixed success to persuade magistrates to deal with my clients leniently and I suppose I have obtained for them a fair share of absolute discharges, conditional discharges and probation orders. There was one occasion, however, after I had been an advocate in magistrates courts for many years when a client of mine was given an absolute discharge which I found difficult to applaud because of the circumstances.

In the reception area of my office I had hung a pair of framed old Denley bank notes on the wall. Rather than stuff them away in a drawer at home, I thought they would be of some interest to my clients if they were on view at the office.

One morning I came into the office and noticed that the frame containing the bank notes was missing. A thorough search was made without success, and it became clear that the notes had been stolen. I had always accepted that there was a chance of this happening but had stubbornly and rather naively entertained a touching faith in the honesty of my clients.

I reported the theft to the police, and within a matter of hours Inspector Harding arrived at my office hotfoot from the station to inform me personally - and finding it hard to keep a straight face - that one of my firm's own clients had been arrested and had admitted the theft. He added with some relish:

'I've been telling you for years about some of your clients, Mr Francis, but you wouldn't believe me, would you?'

Another solicitor was instructed to represent my former client, and he accepted him on the strict understanding that all interviews would be conducted at court and not in his office! At all events he did rather well and persuaded the magistrates to give an absolute discharge.

At the time I felt very annoyed, but on reflection it occured to me that after all those years of persuading the court to give my clients lenient sentences there was an element of poetic justice in being robbed by my own client and that client subsequently receiving an absolute discharge. I did manage to recover one of the bank notes, but the other one had been left in the man's trouser pocket and his mother had put the trousers in the wash!

The Spice of Life

Whilst much of my time as a young advocate was spent in magistrates courts, there were plenty of other venues for litigation of one kind or another. There were tribunals of various kinds - particularly industrial and agricultural ones - there were divorce cases, planning appeals and of course the county court. My philosophy in life is to have a go at as many different things as possible, so I have over the years appeared at just about every type of forum where a solicitor has a right of audience.

Once I attended a court martial to defend a young corporal on a charge of what amounted to a rather bad case of barrack-room bullying. I soon learnt that it doesn't seem to matter what is said at a court martial - the defendant will still receive a very severe sentence!

While the case was on I stayed at the officers' mess and was superbly looked after, but it would have struck an outsider as bizarre in the extreme that the prosecuting officer and myself - who faced each other during the day in very formal surroundings - should every evening dine together in the mess; and what is more, be joined for drinks at the bar by a very lively and thrice-married judge advocate who presided ceremonially over the proceedings, but who at night regaled us at the bar with some very racy and unrepeatable stories!

But I never found any of these forums for litigations anything like as rewarding or interesting as the magistrates court. In the county court, the majority of cases involved building society possession applications, disputed garage bills or claims by finance companies arising from hire purchase agreements. The representatives of the finance companies never seemed to have done their homework or their mathematics correctly, so as often as not their claims did not tally with the figures in their own agreements. On one occasion, another local solicitor and myself set what must have been a record by having to adjourn eleven cases between us so that the figures could be amended.

However, my practice as a country solicitor has been by no means restricted to the drama and ritual of the court room. As I was learning advocacy the hard way I was becoming involved in all the other aspects of general practice - conveyancing, wills, divorces, accident claims, company and commercial work, and generally giving advice to people in trouble. In particular, however, I was becoming involved in agricultural matters and with farmers, for ours was a 'gumboot practice' if ever there was one.

Gumboot Practice

A Law Unto Themselves

Working in a country practice inevitably means dealing with farmers and farming matters, and almost from the word go I involved myself in this part of the firm's work. Although I had spent some time on farms as a boy, and had a smattering of country lore and stockmanship, I still had a lot to learn about farmers.

This fact was forcibly brought home to me the very first time I went to see a farming client. After spending some days cooped up in the office preparing for a major criminal case, I was desperate to get out of the office and into the fresh air. It was a beautiful, sunny day and I called to mind words from the penultimate sentence of *The Amateur Poacher* by Richard Jefferies, words which have always come to me whenever I have felt the 'shades of the prison house' closing around me:

'Let us get out . . . into the sunlight and the pure wind.'

I had a good excuse because a tenant farmer who was a long-established client of the firm had telephoned and asked me to see him at his farm. I left the office and drove through the dale to meet him. The dale had never looked lovelier. It had taken on the pastoral hue which it does for a few precious weeks every summer. The farmer came to the door to greet me, and we stood together in the warm sunshine outside the farmhouse.

'It's a grand view you have from here,' I said.

There was a pause.

'Aye, lad, but it doesn't pay t' bloody rent', he replied.

Talk about being brought back down to earth with a bump. That was my first lesson in dealing with Yorkshire farmers - one which I have never forgotten.

I was to learn a lot more about farmers and farming clients. To start with, most farmers, like country folk generally, are highly suspicious of the law and of legal processes. The best you can hope for is that some of them may learn to respect it. Long explanations of the law to farmers are generally a waste of time and will generally be greeted with a comment like 'It'll be reet' - meaning that if it's that complicated they would sooner sort it out themselves. Clarity and economy of words coupled with succinct advice bluntly delivered are what is required and most appreciated.

The next thing I learnt is that farmers rarely reply to correspondence, particularly in the case of letters sent to them by their bank manager, their inspector of taxes or their solicitor. A telephone call is a better bet, but in the majority of cases there is nothing for it but to put your gumboots in the car and go to see the farmer in person. Country solicitors also soon learn that farmers do not rush to pay their bills and when they eventually do pay they like a bit knocking off, as they would if they were buying a beast at market.

Many of the Dales families have farmed their land for generations, and some can trace their roots back to the Vikings. If they can at times be stubborn and 'ockard', they can also be the most loyal, hospitable and generous of people. They will frequently quarrel amongst themselves, yet in times of trouble they help and support each other. This unity is achieved by the farming community in the face of diversity as well as adversity, for there is as much difference between, say, a sheep farmer and a pig farmer as there is between sheep and pigs.

There is certainly all the difference in the world between the characteristically gentle Dales farmer and his rather rough counterpart who farms around the edges of the industrial West Riding. To state this is to make no criticism of the latter, for he has to be pretty rough as well as tough to survive in such an environment. What a country solicitor must accept and appreciate is that farmers are, above all other clients, a law unto themselves.

The Eighth Wonder of The World

Arguments between neighbouring farmers help to keep a country practice going. There used to be two farming families not so far from Denley who were good examples of this comforting fact.

My client Joe and his neighbour Albert were typical blunt-speaking, proud and independent Yorkshiremen who both had an 'ockard' streak in them. They argued incessantly about anything and everything - about trespassing sheep, about boundary fences, about the obstruction of the flow of spring water and finally they nearly came to blows over the question of which of them was the owner of the long boundary dyke which divided their farms. Both sets of title deeds were examined without either being conclusive, correspondence between solicitors on the subject got nowhere and it was decided to try to resolve the problem by a site meeting. This is not always such a good idea as it seems.

It was a foul day in the middle of November when I put my gumboots in the back of the car and headed for Moor End Farm to meet my counterpart Edward Jackson, an experienced and sensible solicitor with a sense of humour, who represented Albert. We had hoped to meet in the absence of our clients but they insisted on being present at our inspection, even though it was pouring with rain.

We both walked the length of the dyke, a miserable length of peaty water trickling sluggishly between dank, overgrown and weed-infested banks. As we stood, soaked to the skin, and gazing down on a rusty old farm machine which had been abandoned at the bottom of the dyke, Edward Jackson took me on one side:

'Well, Mr Francis, it's not one of the seven wonders of the world, is it?'

At this point our attention was diverted from this doleful sight. Further up the side of the dyke, our clients were obviously arguing, and by the way they were shouting and pointing at each other they were arguing not just about the dyke but about everything they had disagreed upon over the years. We approached to calm them down, but

41

suddenly they both lunged at each other. As they wrestled, they moved towards the edge of the dyke. Suddenly Joe lost his footing in the slippery conditions and fell headlong down the bank, pulling Albert in with him.

Edward Jackson and I, who had stood by in speechless amazement at the goings on, now rushed forward to help them out of the water. We slid down the bank and tried to get them out as best we could, but by the time we had got these two struggling, fully clothed and well-built Dales farmers out of the water we were as wet and muddy as they were.

We all stood there looking at each other for a time. It was Edward Jackson who broke the silence.

'I was just saying to Mr Francis before you fell in that this dyke is not one of the seven wonders of the world.'

The two farmers looked at each other and I guessed they had both reached the same conclusion. They even managed to exchange a knowing grin as they looked at their mud-soaked solicitors.

'Nay', said Joe, shaking his head.

'Nay, it i'n't', replied Albert.

And with that they went on their separate ways back home.

As Jackson as I went back to our cars muddy and sodden, we agreed that Joe and Albert probably wouldn't litigate over the dyke anymore. But we guessed it wouldn't be long either before they found something else to quarrel about.

'And a good thing for our practices' said Edward Jackson cynically.

I smiled and went home to a hot bath.

Time passed and things seemed to have settled down. For a few months I heard nothing from Joe until one day I received a telephone call from him.

'Na then, Mr Francis, that bugger Albert's bin trespassin' agin. Will tha tell us what me reets are at t' law?'

This sounded like a leading question if ever I heard one and I felt uneasy.

'Well Joe, you'd better tell me exactly what has happened, but in general terms if the trespass can be proved you can apply to the court for an injunction, which is a court order restraining him from any further trespass, and you can sue him for the cost of any damage he has caused.'

'Can't I do owt else?'

My unease increased.

'No you can't, Joe. You've asked me what your legal rights are and I've told you that your remedy for trespass is an application to the court.'

'In that case', he replied, 'I'd 'appen best unlock t'mistal an' let t' bugger out.'

'What?'

'Well, I caught 'im snoopin' an' pokin' round t' out'ouses so I locked 'im in t' mistal.'

There was a minute's pause as I took in this revelation and tried to come to terms with my client's action.

'Yes, you let him out, Joe, you do that this instant', I eventually advised. 'I've told you before, you can't take the law into your own hands.'

There was an audible sigh of disappointment from the other end of the phone before Joe rang off.

As a matter of courtesy I decided to phone Edward Jackson. I told him what had happened, that his client was about to be released from my client's cowshed and that he would be getting a call from Albert at any time.

'Not those two again', he said. 'Some things never change.'

Edward and I were obviously set to do battle once again on behalf of our respective clients, but on that one point at least we would agree.

'You're absolutely right', I replied. 'Some things never change'.

The Sale of a Pony

Being a farmers' solicitor has meant that I have often been consulted on problems arising from their commercial transactions. Thus they consult me when their animal feedstuffs are not up to scratch, when their heating systems for poultry or whatever don't work properly or when they invest in machinery which turns out to be defective in some way. They consult me again when the man who buys the old Land Rover which breaks down wants his money back, or when they sell stock which for one reason or another does not satisfy the buyer.

In one of my first court cases I represented a farmer who found himself in court following the sale of a pony to a private customer. The customer was unhappy about the condition of the pony, and if he had complained direct to the farmer no doubt my client would have taken the pony back and made a refund or come to some arrangement. Instead the customer made a complaint to the local authority that the pony was not in as good and sound condition as had been advertised, and after investigating the matter the authority subsequently brought a prosecution under the Trades Descriptions Act.

My client was satisfied that the pony was in good condition when it was sold and that any deterioration must have been caused by the customer not looking after it properly. This was perfectly feasible as there had been an interval of at least two months between the sale of the pony and the complaint to the local authority. So, I advised my client to contest the summons which had been issued against him. I also proceeded to take statements from a number of witnesses who were all prepared to testify as to the excellent condition of the pony prior to the sale.

By the time the case came to trial I was able to call no less than seven witnesses on my client's behalf, among them the local vet who had attended the pony from time to time and knew it well. The case was heard by a stipendiary magistrate and lasted most of the day. When all the evidence had been given, the magistrate addressed me:

'Mr Francis, I have heard from all the witnesses and I do not consider it necessary for you to address me.'

This seemed to be a pretty broad hint that he had made up his mind. He then gave his judgement and in dismissing the case against my client - which I expected - he gave the reason for his decision, a reason which I did not expect at all.

'On the day the pony was sold', the magistrate concluded, 'the defendant gave evidence that his two children were looking out of the window and both were in tears when the pony was being led away from the farm. I am satisfied on this account alone that there was nothing wrong with the pony that day and that its sale was made genuinely and with regret'.

All that carefully prepared submission, all those defence witnesses and all that research and preparation were as nought in their effect compared with the tears of my client's children. I learnt then and I was to go on learning throughout my career as an advocate that you can never be confident about predicting the outcome of any court case - still less can you predict the grounds upon which courts make decisions. If, however, a client's case is won either for wrong or unexpected reasons what does it matter to his lawyer? Still more important, what does it matter to that client? After all, a case won is a case won.

'There's Things Growing in it'

Old Arthur Rigton came to a rather sad end. Like his father and grandfather before him, he had farmed a smallholding all his life and now he was the last of the Rigtons to run the family farm. For Arthur had never married and in his later years had been looked after by his widowed sister. He had never made much money as a farmer, not for the want of working or trying, for he always worked from dawn to dusk seven days a week, rarely taking a holiday. But with his limited acreage, which he farmed in an old-fashioned way, he could only produce so much and he was constantly under pressure from his bank manager.

Not that Arthur allowed these problems to get him down. Like many small, independent-minded farmers he simply tightened his belt a little more when the going got tough. Farming for him and for others like him was quite simply a way of life. Even in the face of the greatest disaster, like seeing his entire herd put down because of foot-and-mouth disease, he remained stubbornly philosophical.

'It's one of them things', he said. 'I'll 'appen 'ave to start all ovver agin.'

I had known Arthur and his farm since I was a boy. The farm was situated in a particularly favoured part of the lower dale and was a child's delight because it contained a bit of everything. There was a herd of Friesian cattle, a flock of fine Masham sheep, some pigs outside, free range hens and a small herd of British Alpine goats which were Arthur's pride and joy.

But the main attraction for me lay at the bottom end of the farm. Here where the land was at its most fertile was an old-fashioned hay meadow and fields put to the plough to grow a little wheat and barley. Alongside them ran a stream where I was allowed to fish for trout when I came to the farm in school holidays to do odd jobs for him - feeding the hens, cutting down thistles, helping at haytime and so on.

I fancy Arthur got as much pleasure from seeing me catching fish from his stream as I got in actually landing them, but what delighted him even more as he sat on the bank upstream from me was spotting dippers and moorhens, dragonflies and water voles and - best of all - glimpsing a sudden brilliant flash of colour which meant there was a kingfisher on his stream. For Arthur was of that fast-vanishing generation of farmers who were also sportsmen and naturalists, the kind of people who in my opinion make the best conservationists.

How on earth old Arthur managed to do all the many different jobs on his livestock-cum-arable farm with only the help of his sister, one part-time man and some seasonal help from lads in the village I will never know. But run the farm he did and still he had time to observe and appreciate his land and its wildlife in all its moods and seasons. For in the same way that I had known and loved every nook and cranny of the old manor house where I had been brought up, so old Arthur loved every field, every stick and stone, every flower and every tree on his farm.

If the daily routine on the farm brought its own reward and satisfaction, what brought real contentment to his life were the simple pleasures, the kind which have delighted all countrymen and naturalists through the ages. Pleasures like seeing a covey of partridges rising from his field, savouring the scent of honeysuckle and new-mown hay, just sitting quietly on the bank of his dipper-haunted trout stream or - his favourite - striding out with a basket on his arm to gather field mushrooms on one of those magical misty mornings in early September.

When I qualified as a solicitor, Arthur's farm hadn't changed much since I had first visited it as a boy. Mains electricity and inside toilets had replaced the old windmill generator and chemical outside lavatories but otherwise the farm was pretty much as it had always been. Arthur had become one of my first clients and it was always a pleasure for me to visit him in his untidy but cosy old-fashioned farmhouse, and I never dreamed of talking business until he had taken me on a conducted tour of the farm and had pointed out any changes since my last visit. His love of wildlife on the farm remained undiminished and he was always particularly keen to tell me about any bird, animal or insect he had seen on the farm for the first time.

'Well, I'm fair capp'd', he would say, as if he felt his small farm had been honoured by such a visit.

Back in his farm kitchen, as we warmed ourselves over the fire with a mug of tea apiece, he would lean forward to me and say, 'It's a reet grand life'. Then and only then would I venture to talk business.

I had not seen Arthur for some months following the death of his sister, and when he asked me to call to draw up a new will I was shocked not only by the change in him but also in the sadly deteriorated state of the farmhouse and land. He had been devoted to his sister and since her death he had let everything go. Seemingly he had lost the will to live. It therefore came as no surprise to me when I heard a couple of months later that he had died.

45

I have always found two things unbearably sad as a solicitor. One is to attend the funeral of a client who has outlived all relatives and friends so that I am the only person there; the second is to see the forced sale of a family farm due to bankruptcy or where the last of the family had died.

Arthur's only surviving relative was an elderly female cousin who lived in Devon. I spoke to her on the telephone and arranged that we would meet at the farm when the weather and her health permitted. In the meantime she instructed me to dispose of Arthur's car so I arranged for Denley Motors to collect the car from the farm. A few days later I received a phone call from their manager, Bill Hamilton. He sounded very serious and very worried.

'Mr Francis, have you seen this car lately?'

I told him I hadn't but knew it had been standing outside for some months unused.

'Mechanically it's fine, but did you know that it's got things growing in it?'

I laughed, but Bill still sounded desperately worried.

'Alright,' I said, 'you'll just have to clean it up as best you can and then get the best price you can'.

Later that day I walked round to the garage to look at the car. Sure enough the inside was sprouting an incredible variety of fungi and grasses. Their spores must have entered the car during its long stand in the open air. Bill grinned an 'I told you so' grin as he saw my own look of astonishment.

'You're right, Bill', I said, 'there are things growing in it'.

It wasn't only Arthur's car which had things growing in it, for when I visited his farm shortly afterwards I looked upon a scene of wilderness and desolation. How quickly, I reflected, can a farm - or a garden for that matter - go to rack and ruin.

As I turned away and remembered Arthur and the farm in their heyday I reminded myself of my own philosophy in life, namely that it is never wise or very sensible either to look back too much or look forward too far. In any case there would be work in plenty waiting for me back at the office.

Of Ducks and Dogs

It is always said that actors avoid being on stage with children and animals. Sometimes they don't have to be even on the stage to cause chaos.

I vividly remember as a boy being taken to see *The Desert Song* or some such other delightful musical at Scarborough's open air theatre, staged on an island in the middle of a lake. There we sat with our blankets and thermos flasks on a chill northern summer evening. Deathly silence always reigned when the lead soprano came on stage to sing her principal melody. As a hush fell upon the audience, the silence would suddenly be broken by a loud 'quack, quack, quack' from ducks swimming round the lake close to the stage.

I think that even the schoolboys in the audience - including me - who tended to find trilling sopranos giggle-making anyway, really felt for her as she struggled to retain her dignity and sing against the quacking of the ducks. Lawyers can place themselves in similar jeopardy.

I have on a number of occasions represented clients who have been charged with keeping a dangerous dog. The preparation of such cases invariably means a visit to the owner's premises, coupled with an inspection of the dog in question at uncomfortably close quarters. Such premises are generally not a surburban house but a farm or smallholding out in the wilds, so the visit usually involves a bumpy drive down a three mile muddy cart track, a precarious walk across a farmyard full of muck, nettles, weeds, scrap iron, junky old tractors and other farming accessories, to be followed by a discussion with the client which usually goes something like this:

'Tha's come to look at t'dog, ave yer?'

'Yes', I say somewhat nervously, knowing it to have bitten a number of people on previous ocasions.

'Well, come ovver 'ere then.'

I hesitate.

'Na don't look sae freetened, it'll not touch thee.'

'Are you quite sure about that?', I ask even more nervously.

'Ah keeps kellin' thee, Mr Francis, our Rex wouldn't 'urt a fly.'

As the dog's eyes meet mine and bares his teeth as he looks me over, I find myself struggling to agree with my client.

I was involved in one such case where my client's dog had bitten several people who had been innocent visitors to his farm. Because there had been a previous court order

for the dog to be kept under proper control, this time the magistrates had ordered the dog to be destroyed. My client instructed me to appeal against this decision to the Quarter Sessions (the appropriate legal forum in those days). Moreover my client took the enormous gamble of insisting, against my advice, that the dog be taken to court with him.

An eloquent plea was made by counsel on my client's behalf during his summing up.

'You have heard the evidence about the behaviour of this dog from the owner, how it is a family pet and how greatly loved by all in the local community, but most important of all you have had the opportunity of seeing the dog in court, and just how well-behaved and loveable he really is.'

47

The dog was indeed quiet and well-behaved throughout. Too well-behaved, I remember thinking. There was a respectful silence in court for the chairman to announce the court's decision. Just as he started to speak the silence was broken by a very loud barking. The dog suddenly jumped up, and before anyone could do anything, it made straight for the chairman and bit his hand. There was total chaos in court for a few minutes before order was restored. My client's appeal was, I seem to remember, dismissed!

The Great Pig Chase

At one time or another I have kept most kinds of farm animals, but I have not as yet tried my hand with pigs. However I have acted for several pig farmers and have been party to several cases involving their stock.

The very first time I went to the magistrates court was when I was an articled clerk and my principal, Phillip Lytton, was defending a local licensee for selling drink after hours. The police had raided his premises at the dead of night and found him serving drinks to three worthy locals, Fred, Arthur and Charlie. The licensee had a pig farm adjoining his pub and his defence was that Fred, Arthur and Charlie were not customers at all but his good friends who had come to help him castrate the pigs. This was thirsty work and they all needed a drink when it was over. The police didn't believe him but the magistrates did and the case was dismissed.

'Do you think it had anything to with a local farmer being chairman of the bench?', I had asked Phillip Lytton after the case.

'You shouldn't be so cynical at your age', he answered with a grin.

In my early years of legal practice there were a number of investment schemes which were popular with the general public. One such scheme was an invitation to the public to invest in a pig farming enterprise, the idea being that the farmer did all the work but the investor would share in the hoped-for progeny of the pig or pigs in which he had invested. The investors attracted to this scheme were, for the most part, outsiders or city types. The locals knew better.

One day I received a telephone call from a rather superior-sounding London solicitor who told me that a client of his had invested a considerable amount of money in one of these pig schemes at a farm in Yorkshire, and although over two years has passed since the investment was made his client had not received a penny. I told him I would make some enquiries on his behalf and report back.

I found out that the company which had been set up to run the scheme was heavily in debt and likely to go into liquidation at any moment. I decided that the only hope of salvaging anything from the imminent wreck was to employ some fairly rapid self-help. I promptly visited the farm and found the farmer in a depressed state of mind.

When I explained the reason for my visit he said, 'Well you'd best tek what you can get, lad, there's eight piglets ovver theer, t' rest are gone or spoken for.'

Now my London solicitor's client had a quarter stake in a grown pig, so I reckoned

if I got two piglets for him it would be about right. With the help of the farmer I managed to get them into my car and drove back to Denley.

I telephoned the posh London solicitor, and putting on my broadest Yorkshire accent I said:

'Na then, A've not gitten thy pig, but A've gitten two piglets for thee. Wheer dust tha want 'em tekkin?'

There was a long silence.

As my old friend Arthur Rigton would have said, he was obviously 'fair capped'. Eventually he managed a nervous laugh.

'Well I've really no experience of this sort of thing, Mr Francis, what do you suggest?'

Resuming my normal voice, I suggested that he should leave it to me to contact the local auction mart to make the necessary arrangements. My London friend speedily agreed to this suggestion. His fright at the prospect of having to take charge of two wild piglets had receded.

There was another occasion not long afterwards when I came into close contact with pigs. I was defending a pig farmer in one of the local magistrates' courts in a road traffic case. Just as my client was giving evidence the case was suddenly interrupted by a very worried looking court official who told us that a pig was running loose in the court car park.

My client's face fell. He had put one of his pigs in the back of the van and he had failed to shut the door properly. The result - one escaped pig.

The court adjourned for a few minutes to enable my client, assisted by a motley collection of court officials, solicitors, magistrates, police and members of the public, to catch his pig and secure it in a van ready to take to market. After a few circuits of the car park, and after some difficulty, our combined efforts were successful.

When the court resumed, my client was still red-faced, panting and unable to give evidence. I had to seek a further adjournment for him to compose himself. Come to think of it we all needed a further adjournment to compose ourselves, not just because we were out of breath but because we were all still laughing.

'There's No Bugger Theer'

There is always an element of anticipation and excitement at a sale by public auction, particularly when it is held in a Dales village where it is looked on as something of a social occasion. Apart from the auctioneer, the vendor's solicitor has to attend in order to read out the contract and the sale conditions.

For the solicitor it can be a worrying time in case he should be faced with an awkward question about the property by one of the locals, who may well know rather more about the history and use of the property than he does.

'What about t' watter reights?', 'Dust tha know wheer t'septic tank is?' or 'Who's wall is it at t'back o' yon mistal?' are the sort of questions likely to trip up the unprepared solicitor.

His first job, however, is to remember to go to the right place on the right day for the auction. Twice I have nearly come unstuck by failing on these essentials.

The first time I had got the auction down in my diary for the wrong date. Sitting in my office one day I received a panicky telephone call from the auctioneer to say that about two hundred people were patiently awaiting my arrival at The George Hotel and was I coming? Luckily the contract was already prepared and I dashed straight off to the sale, which eventually got under way nearly an hour late.

The second time the auction was being held at a village hall which I had never been to before. When I arrived there seemed to be an exceptionally large number of cars in the car park and the inside of the hall was full of women. I was slightly puzzled and asked one of the women whether I was in the right place for the sale.

'No', she laughed, 'the sale is being held in the room at the back. You're in the room where the ladies keep-fit class is about to start.'

I smiled and left rather quickly.

Of course it is not only solicitors who can have problems at auction sales, auctioneers can get into difficulties too. There was a sale I attended at a pub up the dale, and most of the locals, mainly farmers, had turned out for it. Big crowd though there may have been, there was only one serious bidder for the property, which is not that unusual, particularly if the property market is depressed. In order to try to get his price the auctioneer resorted to what is known in the trade as 'bouncing bids off the wall'. The bid was 'raised' three times - each time by the auctioneer himself.

Now it has been said many times that 'you can always tell a Yorkshireman but you can't tell him much', and Charley Blackburn, who was bidding for the property, was certainly no fool. Having seen his own bid raised on three occasions, he demanded that the auctioneer tell him who was bidding against him.

The auctioneer stumbled and stammered, and Charley turned triumphantly and indignantly to the crowd as he said 'I tell thee, there's no bugger theer.'

By now the crowd were getting behind him.

'Tha's reet, Charley, there's no bugger theer.'

Chaos and confusion reigned for a short time until the auctioneer withdrew the property from the market and beat a hasty and undignified retreat. If at any time in the future that auctioneer should become too cocky or feel clever at 'bouncing bids off the wall', someone should just whisper to him, be it ever so softly, 'there's no bugger theer'.

The Midas Touch

One of Charley's neighbours, a farmer called Abe Murgatroyd, was a client of mine. If Charley was no fool, Abe was not noted for his generosity. In fact it was variously said of him either that he wouldn't give you the weight of a cigarette end or that he'd split a currant. Certainly Abe only had two discernible interests in life: one was money and the other was brass.

To look at Abe anyone would have thought that he hadn't two ha'pennies to rub together. Dressed in a pair of scruffy old corduroys, a dirty tattered shirt and a pullover torn and full of holes and with a funny little woollen hat over his head, he looked more like a tramp than a prosperous farmer.

This was all part of his deception. When it came to business, Abe assuredly had the Midas touch. His farm was his base but he didn't 'mek 'is brass' there. That came from dealing - and when it came to dealing Abe had no equal in his dale. He seemed to know the market for everything from scrap iron and farm implements to furniture and antique china. He could buy and would buy anything and everything from anybody, sell it and make a profit on it.

But his real speciality lay in his land and property speculations. If any neighbouring farm came onto the market it was likely as not that Abe would buy it, resell the farmhouse and some of the land and then keep the rest of the land for himself. That way he added to his acreage at little or no cost to himself.

But Abe's property speculations were by no means confined to his own locality. Leaving his sons to look after the farm, he often went off to various parts of the country looking to make a killing on some property speculation, and it was in this field, so to speak, that his genius lay. Abe always seemed to manage to buy that bit of land which was essential for access to a new road development or that little terrace home which stood in the way of some major planning project. When Abe held the key to such developments he did not let go of it cheaply.

Abe's neighbours and fellow villagers were well aware of his activities. In the close-knit Dales communities, success and failure, generosity and meanness are common knowledge. Certainly Abe's operations were well-known and he was respected rather than liked. One day, after yet another of his successful business coups, I had been at his farm completing the paperwork and he suggested - in typical fashion - that I might like to buy him a pint at his local to celebrate his success.

The bar was packed out. I bought a drink for Abe and myself and after we had finished there was a long pause. Whether it was the immediate effect of the pint of bitter, the accumulated effect of years of Abe's meanness and waiting months for my bills to be paid I don't know, but I suddenly resolved that somehow or other I was going to get Abe to do something he had never been known to do before - stand a round of drinks.

I waited till there was a slight lull in the noise of the pub, and remembering the words of an old Yorkshireman I had once known, I said as deliberately and loudly as I dared:

'Now then Abe, I've supped up, have I done right?'

There was silence for a minute, then all the locals joined in.

'Come on Abe lad, we've all supped up, 'ave we dun reet an' all?'

Slowly, very slowly, Abe put his hands in his pockets, and with a look of utter anguish, produced some brass and actually paid for a round of drinks.

Abe never did forgive me for that, but if I lost one client that afternoon, I think I won quite a few more!

'To 'ell wi' 'ectares!'

Not that it should be supposed for one minute that Abe Murgatroyd was a typical Dales farmer. In fact he was highly untypical.

My good friend and client Bobby Hebden was a much truer example of his kind. Apart from his great love of nature and the land, Bobby's interests lay in shooting, cricket and bee-keeping. I had known Bobby since I was old enough to place decoys near the wood where he taught me to shoot pigeons, since I was old enough to watch him admiringly as he smote mighty sixes for his village cricket team and since I was old enough to see him at work with his hives and help him to remove the supers and cut the honey into mouthwatering combs.

Like most Dales farmers, Bobby took some getting to know but once you had won his confidence you had a friend for life. His was a mixed livestock farm with a good milking herd, some sheep and pigs, a large number of free-range hens and a duckpond. He was conservative in all things and highly suspicious of any change in farming practices or methods.

I once remarked to him, 'Well, Bobby, you'll have seen a lot of changes in farming over the years.'

'Aye lad, an' 'ave bin agin 'em all.'

Bobby 'reckoned nowt' to lots of things, to battery hens, to the intensive keeping of calves and pigs, to the increased use of chemicals and pesticides and above all to the switch by so many farmers from hay to silage.

'What's up wi' 'em', he used to say of such farmers, 'when t' sun shines, it meks itsel does 'ay.'

Old-fashioned he may have been but successful he certainly was as the large collection of show-winning rosettes pinned up in his barn eloquently testified.

As well as being old-fashioned, he had the typical Dales way of talking to his fellow farmers. One day I was driving back with him from the twice-weekly Denley cattle market when his view of the main road ahead was obscured by a group of farmers, standing in the middle of the road chatting and generally passing the time of day. Bobby brought his battered old van to a halt, leaned out of the window and said:

'Tha meks a better door than winder.'

Like most of the older generation of Dalesfolk, he had great difficulty in understanding that so many city folk - 'off-comed uns' he called them - came to the country but didn't really 'see' it or understand it. He once told me of a city type who had approached him as he strolled along the public footpath that ran through his farm.

'Tell me', he said, 'you're a farming chappy aren't you? Well, why do farmers always put their gates in the muddiest part of the field?'

Bobby just shook his head in disbelief as he walked away.

Not surprisingly, Bobby liked yards, shillings and all other things English, so when I once had to get him to fill in a form which asked, among other things, how many hectares he owned there was a violent reaction.

'To 'ell wi 'ectares!', he thundered. 'Tha cun put down that A've gitten a hundred and forty acre an that'll 'ave to do 'em.'

It was the same when the VAT inspector called at the farm.

'This 'ere VAT tha's on about', he said as he eyed the inspector suspiciously, 'well it dun't seem to 'ave caught on reet well around 'ere.'

I greatly sympathised with Bobby and suspect, that just as the British people have rejected centigrade and clung stubbornly to farenheit, so will Dales farmers like Bobby stick to yards and acres rather than metres and hectares.

Bobby died suddenly of a heart attack when he was out shooting pigeons. It was the way he would have chosen to go, but for his wife and family it came as a tremendous shock. Bobby's wife Joan had been an ideal farmer's wife. Being the daughter of a farmer herself she had known exactly what was expected of her. Apart from bringing up four strapping lads she had cooked, baked, knitted and sewed, washed and ironed, had helped on the farm where she was capable of doing anything from milking the cows to driving the tractor, and had catered for paying guests in the summer to help out with the money.

Now, for the first time in her life, Joan found she couldn't cope. It wasn't working the farm that was the problem as her boys looked after that - it was the business side which defeated her because she had no experience of it. When Bobby had been alive he had seen to all that.

When I went to see Joan soon after Bobby's death I was horrified to find that she had made provisional arrangements to sell some household contents for £500 to a dealer who had called at the farm after reading her husband's obituary notice in the local paper. I am no expert on antiques and paintings, but included in the contents to be sold was an oil painting which I suspected was alone worth more than £500.

I managed to persuade Joan that, if she really had to sell some of their things to raise some cash, she should put them in a saleroom. I was relieved that she agreed, particularly when at the sale which followed the painting alone fetched £4,500. Joan never looked back after that and with the help of her lads the farm went from strength to strength.

To draft a difficult lease or conveyance well or to win a court case is of course satisfactory to any lawyer, but surely more rewarding by far is to be in a position to give advice to people in times of trouble and to protect them from the ruthless or the unscrupulous of this world. To be able to help the weak and vulnerable is one of the privileges of being a family solicitor.

Helping Hands

It must have been all those farming clients and all those trips to farms with my gumboots in the back of the car which inspired me, but after a year or two in practice I decided to go in for a bit of farming myself on a small scale.

My wife Rosemary and I had bought an old cottage in a moorland village not far from

Denley and, after we had got the cottage the way we wanted it, we turned our attention to the acre field which went with it. We decided to try to become as self-sufficient as possible. Some years later, self-sufficiency was to become fashionable following the series *The Good Life* on television. I noticed country people found this fashion rather amusing, presumably because they had been self-sufficient for years without needing to give it a fancy name or make a fuss about it.

I started by making a vegetable plot out of part of the field, and on the fine virgin soil I soon had plenty of green vegetables, potatoes and other root crops. Even at our high altitude I managed to coax a few strawberries, raspberries and currants to fruit.

Rosemary and I then debated what animals we were going to keep. We already had a magnificent English pointer which had been given to us as a wedding present, and a local cat had adopted us and presented us with kittens. There was also a noisy budgie in the kitchen. But these were just pets. What farm animals would take us down the road of self-sufficiency?

After careful thought we decided that goats would be right for our rough land, and off we went to see a farmer who had advertised several for sale. Both of us had been country children, and we both knew a little of stock and of farming, but that we knew nothing about goats was soon to be dramatically proved. The farmer showed us two goats, one a pedigree Saanen and the other a rather small scrub goat. We chose the latter principally because she looked so appealing and had a nice face. What we should of course have been looking for in our first goat was a good milker, not a pet with a nice face. No wonder the farmer was smiling when we paid him and left.

The next day when I came home from the office, Rosemary was in tears. She had spent over half an hour trying to milk Peggy, as we had called her. The bottom of the pail was barely covered with milk and then the stupid animal had stepped in it and done her business in it.

'Never mind, things can only get better,' I said hopefully.

Slowly as we learnt by our mistakes things did get better. We didn't keep Peggy for very long but soon afterwards we acquired two splendid Saanens called Margaret and Meleia and - my own favourite - a blue British Alpine cross with a liking for the smell of pipe tobacco whom we called Bluebell. They were all three excellent milkers, and my wife and I gradually improved our milking technique. We could hardly fail with the constant practice we were getting!

Each goat, or rather each teat on each goat, being different we had to keep swapping the goats we milked to make sure that Margaret and Meleia would allow themselves to be milked by me as well as my wife, and so that Bluebell who readily accepted me would also accept a female milker.

Soon we had pints of milk every day. Now goat's milk when fresh is really excellent, and we never told our visitors that the milk we gave them with their tea was goat's milk, and they never noticed. None of the gallons of milk which we produced was wasted, although I do seem to remember having an awful lot of milk puddings at that time!

To the goats we gradually added a dozen hens, a few ducks and a couple of hives of bees. The latter produced some fine heather honey which we ate with my wife's home-made bread and fresh butter made in the village. Now that was a feast fit for the gods. Any spare bits of honey and comb we used up in making bottles of mead to keep us happy in the winter. I think you are supposed to leave mead for at least five years, but we could never wait that long.

We built up quite a menagerie one way and another. There was a lot of hard work but it was all great fun and very rewarding.

However our life looking after farm stock and trying to be self-sufficient was not without its problems. One of the most serious of these was overcome with the assistance of one of my farming clients. My wife was determined to build up a pedigree herd of goats and to this end she had, on no less than three occasions, taken Meleia, our fine Saanen, to a pedigree billy some considerable distance away. Alas nothing happened and Meleia was not in kid.

I thought about the problem for a while and then remembered that one of my nearby farming clients, Jimmy Dacre, owned a billy goat.

'I think you will have to give up the idea of a pedigree herd', I said to Rosemary, 'but if you will leave it to me I'm pretty sure I know someone who can help us.'

Jimmy came up to our place one dark wet evening with his large, dirty and rather smelly scrub billy goat. After putting him to Meleia, he said to Rosemary:

'Na then, missus, it'll be bingo fust time round, Ah reckons.'

Sure enough, it was bingo first time. Meleia duly produced two delightful but definitely non-pedigree kids and was very soon in full milk again. Clients can come in useful sometimes, I thought.

But it wasn't just my farming clients who helped us with the problems of running a smallholding. In Tommy and Bet we were blessed with the best neighbours any young married couple could have had.

Tommy was a living embodiment of that old Tyke saying, 'If tha wants owt doin' well, do it thisen'. There was no practical job he could not do - and do with the skill of a born craftsman and countryman - whether it was building, walling, plumbing, scything, tree felling, mole catching or any job to do with stock or the land on his own small hill farm.

He was wonderfully skilled in working with any kind of material and possessed a rare ability to carve wooden objects, particularly animals, out of odd pieces of wood, shaping them with simple tools so that they appeared miraculously true to life. Around his cottage there were always lots of wooden models - a friend's favourite dog, a neighbouring farmer's sheep or a village pet lamb. At Tommy's side was always his wife Bet, skilled in all the traditional homemaking arts of the countrywoman , who with their 'lads' was always ready to give a hand around the farm when help was needed.

Tommy and Bet rejoiced with us in our successes, comforted us in our disappointments, kept a quiet eye on us without interfering, encouraged us in our efforts and made sure that we didn't make too many serious mistakes with either our stock or our land.

These were happy days and I shall never forget the year Tommy, Bet and 'the lads' came to 'help' us with haymaking in our field and we made it the old-fashioned way. Rather they made it with a little help from ourselves. After Tommy had mowed the grass, left it to dry, turned it and turned it again, he divided the working party into two gangs. The first gang, of which I was a member, gathered the hay into rows using large wooden-pronged rakes whilst the second gang pulled the rows into small pikes called 'cocks'. These were in turn forked into large pikes which were then led into the barn.

It was a blazing hot summer's day when we completed the work and I don't think until that day I had ever before really appreciated the literal truth of the old proverb 'make hay while the sun shines', for when hay is made under such conditions it 'dries green', as they say, and fills the air with a scent of such sweetness as to banish all anxiety for the winter feeding of stock.

As we led the last of the hay from our field and enjoyed a few refreshing drinks in the moonlight, Tommy, who was not given to paying idle complimemts, said a few words to me which I shall treasure all my life:

'You can be one of our gang any time you like.'

I had only played a small labouring part in Tommy's production - and played it with only a fraction of his skill - but those few words meant as much to me as winning any court case or solving the most intractable legal problem.

Tommy and Bet still live on the same hill farm and when I visit them to talk and reminisce and just to enjoy their company, I find that Tommy has lost none of his skill in country crafts or in his wood carving.

It is, however, as a hill farmer that I shall always think of him, for he is one of a special breed. To survive as a hill farmer in our hardy northern climate you must, I think, have been brought up on it or at least have experienced the life for a good many years. Whenever I think of Tommy I see him dressed in a heavy coat and muffler against the elements, but with a cheerful smile on his weather-beaten face, striding up the hill across his land. This was always where he best liked to be, the sort of place in Emily Bronte's words:

'Where the grey flocks in ferny glens are feeding,
Where the wild wind blows on the mountain side.'

My farming clients, and looking after my own smallholding, were taking up quite a lot of my time, but I had many other interests as well. In particular there was sport, and nothing in my life has ever kept me for long from my abiding love of sport. I have had quite a number of sporting clients as well, and they, like every client, have a story to tell too.

This Sporting Life

Playing the Game

'Work hard and play hard' was a favoured and oft-repeated piece of advice given by headmasters to schoolboys of my generation. We were constantly urged to 'play the game' both on and off the field. I have always believed that man should not live by work alone and have attempted at one time or another, with varying degrees of success, to play most sports.

The two exceptions which immediately spring to mind are croquet, which I am saving for my old age, and polo, or 'chukka' as the exponents of the game call it. Mind you, we had our own version of 'chukka' as children. It was played on bikes rather than horses and it led to shocking damage to our prize rosebed when we rode our bikes into it off the lawn at breakneck speed.

As for 'playing the game', sadly it seems to me that sportsmanship and gentlemanly behaviour are hardly compatible with the attitude of some modern professional sportsmen who seem to be prepared to stoop to any lengths in order to win, whether it is by taking drugs, by intimidation and abuse of opponents or officials or by other deliberate breaches of the rules, called 'professional fouls'. In plain language they are cheats and it seems to me that a victory won by cheating is no real victory at all.

When I was at prep school there was a cup awarded each year to the boy who by the vote of his fellow pupils had best 'played the game both on and off the field'. Winning that trophy one year meant every bit as much to me as gaining a scholarship or captaining the football and cricket teams.

There are businessmen and solicitors in the big cities who spend nearly all their time working. It is little wonder to me that so many of these workaholics feel as if life is passing them by. As far as solicitors are concerned, what a limited experience of life they must have to draw on when advising their clients.

I am old-fashioned enough to believe that 'work hard and play hard' is a good slogan when coupled with that other saying that 'variety is the spice of life'. Specialisation can be carried too far and can result in tunnel vision. Wisdom and humanity are much more likely to come from a rich and varied life.

I have certainly enjoyed variety in my work as a country solicitor, but at the same time I have made sure that my sporting life has continued unabated. I have found that just as it helps to have a little knowledge of agriculture and rural customs when it comes to talking to farming clients, so it also helps to have a sporting background when talking to clients who are sportsmen themselves or who are involved in sport in some way, even if it is only to talk about the local football team or the fortunes of Yorkshire cricket.

Funnily enough one of my first cases in the office was to do with sport, or more specifically with an amateur football club. It was a case which I inherited from Cyril Boothroyd, the senior partner in the firm who was then about to retire and be succeeded by Philip Lytton.

Before he retired, Cyril had been involved in the administration of amateur football in the county for many years, although paradoxically he had never to my knowledge kicked a football in his life. The case I inherited from him was one in which there had been a dispute in one of the clubs where the secretary had refused to accept his own dismissal - and had also refused to hand over the club's book of accounts and other documents. Fortunately the threat of court proceedings eventually persuaded him to do so.

Most people might not expect amateur sporting clubs to be associated with resignations, disputes and litigation, but of all voluntary bodies they are, in my experience, the most susceptible to rows of one kind or another - followed closely by church committees and amateur dramatic societies. It all makes work for the lawyer, I suppose, but whether it's the kind of work he wants to get involved in, particularly if he is a member of those bodies, is quite another matter!

Not long after this incident, I was instructed to act on behalf of the Norcross Sports Society Committee. Their annual gala had been losing support for several years, and the last year had been a total disaster as it had rained all day. This was the last straw. The committee lost heart and decided to disband.

As I read through the society's records, I discovered that the constitution drafted in 1893 provided for just such an eventuality, since it specified that any surplus assets after disbandment should be distributed among 'the poor of Norcross'.

Now the gala had accumulated a bob or two over the years, and the problem facing the committee, and myself as their legal adviser, was how best to comply with the requirements of the constitution. Quite a few members of the society, among them some very substantial farmers and prosperous members of the local community, then tried to convince me that they were all numbered among 'the poor of Norcross', and so should have a share in the money.

I eventually solved the problem by advising the committee that the assets could perhaps be used to set up a prize at the village school for the most promising athlete each year, either to buy sports equipment or to train with a professional coach for a few days. Everyone in Norcross seemed happy with my solution, particularly when only a couple of years later one young schoolgirl was chosen to represent the county junior athletics team.

After being in practice for no more than a year, apart from sorting out the problems of several amateur football associations, I had acted for a surprising number of sportsmen - including several professional footballers - sportswomen, officials, a couple of golfers, league cricketers, tennis players and a variety of country sportsmen of one kind or another. My love and knowledge of sport has been made immeasurably richer by my association with my sporting clients and friends, an association which I have always valued both in and out of the office.

Best of all Games

I suppose that over the years I have spent nearly as much time on tennis courts as in the law courts. Whenever I tell my secretary that I have to leave the office for an appointment at any time between April and October, she strongly suspects - or knows by now - that there is a reasonable chance I am off to play in a tennis match.

Whenever I think of tennis, my favourite of all games, I remember with affection my first club with its small wooden pavilion and the members making tea on a Sunday afternoon. But before I had even joined a tennis club I was practising against our garden wall and playing on the grass court we were lucky enough to have at home.

It was my job at the start of every season to get out the encyclopaedia, check the measurements (which I never could remember), cut and roll the lawn and finally to mark it out in brilliant white. It was a tricky job to keep a straight line, but an even trickier job to get the whitening to just the right consistency. Our tennis lawn was not exactly centre court at Wimbledon, not just because I was the chief groundsman but because it also had to double for our cricket test matches, football cup finals, for our bicycle polo and all the other games; but it was a start, it was fun and it kindled my enthusiasm for the sport.

One Major Russell Bunn and his wife Mary used to come from the nearby village of Levenhope to play on our court, and it was a great treat when they invited some of the 'young people', as they called us, to one of their tennis parties at Levenhope Manor, their beautiful seventeenth century house.

There, on a superbly maintained grass court, would stand the major carrying an old green sports bag, immaculately attired in long white flannels, Fred Perry shirt and always with a colourful silk cravat. Next to him would stand his wife, Mary, resplendent in a pristine English white tennis dress, and next to her their gorgeous daughter Elizabeth. She with her splendid tennis legs always reminded me of a younger version of Joan Hunter-Dunn, who was immortalised by the late and much-loved Sir John Betjeman. We adolescent boys worshipped her from afar and parodied the poet laureate's lines:

'Elizabeth Bunn, Elizabeth Bunn,
Furnished and burnished by Levenhope sun.'

Tennis parties at the major's were always special, not least for the splendid afternoon teas which were part of them. What the major and his wife, who have now passed on, would have thought of the modern professional tennis players with their grunting, their spitting, their scowling, their constant questioning and abuse of umpires and officials, and their utter joylesness, I dare not think. I feel sure that the major for his part would have reckoned tennis to have been far better when it was played in white and for fun.

Not that the major himself remained silent on the tennis court. He was constantly shouting encouragement to us:

'Good shot, sir.'
'Well played, that man.'
'That's the style' or 'bend your knees, boy.'

60

Inbetween his loud hearty laugh and his words of encouragement came frequent expletives, but always directed against himself. His worst expletives were 'rubbish', 'balderdash' and 'pathetic', or if he was really cross with himself, 'That shot was the very essence of pathos'!

Tennis at the major's was played seriously but with enjoyment. We learnt a lot about the game from him, but perhaps most valuably we learnt something of fair play, sportsmanship, and gentlemanly behaviour. Certainly if one of us had intentionally cheated, or used obscene language, or hit a ball deliberately at one of the 'gels' as he called them, we would never have been invited to one of his parties again.

Since my first tennis on grass courts I have played on concrete and red shale, on wood and tarmac, on indoor and the modern all-weather courts, and on just about every surface there is. It may be pure nostalgia but grass court tennis is to me still the best, and I shall forever associate it with the smell of newly-mown lawns, the fragrant scent of roses round the court, deck chairs, cucumber sandwiches for tea, and the courtesy and enjoyment of it all.

Mixed Doubles

From my friendly first tennis club and from tennis parties at home and at the major's, I graduated to tournaments and to league tennis. Shortly after I had qualified as a solicitor I joined Denley Tennis Club, whom I have since represented in the local mixed doubles league.

League tennis in our neck of the woods is taken seriously, but not that seriously. It is, after all, not the Tyke's national game. It is in every respect enjoyable but Wimbledon it is not. Surely, however, there can be few more delightful ways of spending a summer's evening then playing mixed doubles at a village club, followed by a get-together and tea and a chat in the pavilion.

In a small club like ours, actually producing a team can be a problem of crisis proportions, and the details of organisation sometimes have a way of being left to chance. There was one evening when we were due to play a match at East Stonebeck, a village club some distance from our own. It was raining intermittently and we were not sure whether to set off or not. However, we hadn't received a phone call and off we all went together in one car. Having got halfway on our journey it was still raining and we decided to stop and telephone to see if the match was still on. We could remember that the surname of the East Stonebeck Club Secretary was a certain Mr Hudson, but for the life of us none of us could think of his first name, his address or his telephone number. We had therefore no choice but to start ringing up all the Hudsons listed in the appropriate telephone directory, beginning each conversation:

'Are you Mr Hudson?'

- and if the answer was 'yes':

'Sorry to trouble you, but are you by chance the tennis Mr Hudson from East Stonebeck?'

There were an awful lot of Hudsons listed in that directory but we were in luck; the fourth out of the list was the tennis Mr Hudson, who told us it had just stopped raining at East Stonebeck and the match was still on.

The adventures of that particular evening were by no means over. The match turned out to be closely contested, and the result finally hinged on whether our third couple, Norman and Moira Dennison, were able to beat East Stonebeck's first pair, Geoffrey and Barbara Blake.

To my mind, husband and wife playing tennis together generally does not make for harmony, but there was an extra ingredient in this match which made for it being a particularly explosive encounter. For, as we all stood watching the 'decider', there was something I knew which the others didn't.

Norman, who was the sole principal of a firm of chartered accountants in Denley, happened to be a long-standing client as well as friend of mine. For several years Geoffrey, his opponent across the net, had worked for him as his assistant accountant. Then one day Geoffrey had suddenly decided he could do better on his own, and without any notice or warning he had walked out on Norman and set up his own offices in premises just across the road - in blatantly direct competition with his old boss.

He had done this in spite of the fact that, under the terms of his contract of employment, he was prohibited from practising within a five mile radius of Denley for a period of five years from leaving the firm. Geoffrey had gambled on Norman doing nothing about it, but Norman was incensed at what he saw as an act of betrayal and instructed me to take Geoffrey to court for breach of contract. This I did, and obtained an injunction preventing Geoffrey from working in Denley.

In order to comply with the court order, Geoffrey had to move to an office many miles further up the dale in East Stonebeck, and had never forgiven Norman for what he considered was the petty spite he had shown towards him by taking him to court. What Norman and I didn't know until that evening was that Geoffrey now played for his local tennis club.

As the players changed ends after the first game, I could just hear Geoffrey saying to Norman:

'It's a different kind of court this time, Dennison, and now it's my turn to win.'

Norman said nothing, but the grim expression on his face made it obvious that he was absolutely determined that this wouldn't happen if he could help it. The two men's wives, who of course both knew of the dispute between the two men, were determined to back them up and kept glaring at each other from opposite ends of the court.

'It's going to be a real needle match', I thought, and I was right.

In the gathering gloom the final set was played out in a heavy drizzle. The players were all exceptionally tense. Every doubtful decision was vehemently disputed, and there were sighs and groans interspersed with muttered curses and anguished cries of 'I didn't see it', 'You jammy beggar, I don't believe it!' and 'Are you sure that ball was out?'

There were sighs - of relief - from us when the match was halved. The tension was broken and, rather in the manner of boxers who embrace each other after a gruelling fight, Norman and Geoffrey shook hands, Moira and Barbara kissed each other and, having restored their frienship, the four of them enjoyed a happy and relaxing after-match tea with the rest of us.

'An honourable draw', I said to myself. 'There's a lot to be said for an honourable draw.'

Apart from actually playing tennis I have always enjoyed encouraging children to learn my favourite game, and several years ago it occured to me that I might be able to put a bit more back into the game which has given me so much pleasure if I qualified as a tennis coach.

To this end I boldly and foolhardily enrolled myself on a tennis coaches' course where I confidently expected to find at least a few club players of my age and vintage. At the first session I was more than a little dismayed to find that there was nobody on the course within twenty years of me. I was surrounded by young PE students and teachers, some of whom who were apparently simply motivated by the need to obtain another paper qualification to go on their CV's. The course tutor was of my generation it is true, but he made it clear right at the start that no allowance whatever would be made for my age.

'Right, everybody collect ten balls from the back of the court and the last one of you back to me does twenty press ups.'

Some chance I had against the young PE students. I did an awful lot of press ups during that course! Somehow, though, I survived until the day of the examination when it poured down with rain and no play was possible on the outside courts. The exam was switched to a nearby gym where benches placed on top of each other were made to represent nets. The group of children with whom I had to demonstrate my coaching powers comprised a mixture of teenage boys, whose main aim was to knock the cover off the ball with every shot, and little girls holding expensive tennis rackets which they could barely lift.

I just about got through the day and the exam, thus fulfilling my ambition to be an elementary tennis coach, but the experience made me think that to coach tennis on a regular basis could be hard work. However, at least I could get the children to collect the balls and I wouldn't have to do any press ups.

I keep wondering every year whether I wish to carry on playing against increasingly younger and more athletic players in league tennis, but when I start to waver I think of Wilf, one of our club members, who is now seventy-four but who plays regularly in winter and summer alike. He effectively counters the power and athleticism of younger players with his marvellous skill, finesse and anticipation. Wilf disclosed to me the other day that he intends to keep playing tennis until he is ninety - then he will take up bowls.

'Now that's the right attitude', I thought.

On the first league tennis match of the season I know from experience that it will be a dark, overcast and chilly April evening, there will be a threat of rain and a cutting, icy-cold wind. It will be an evening when the ladies will wear gloves and the men will carry hip flasks, but I will be happy because by then I will have seen the first small tortoiseshell butterfly, blackbirds will be singing in my garden and there will be celandines, violets and primroses in flower.

With the coming of spring the sap will have already risen within me, so I will remember Wilf's example as I encourage the rest of our rather middle-aged team to do battle. As we sally forth to play mixed doubles once again I will quote Shakespeare, much in the style of my old tennis mentor the major, as I exhort them:

'Once more unto the breach, dear friends, once more'.

The Football

The Lord above may have made man to help his neighbour, but solicitors know that in practice man very often does not. Neighbour disputes of one kind or another are frequently the subject of protracted correspondence between solicitors, and sometimes end up in court.

Very often the issues involved in such cases are plainly not worth the trouble and expense incurred, and of course the parties still have to live next door to each other after the case whatever the result. Most of these cases revolve around arguments about boundaries, fences, shared drives, rights of way and unsightly developments, but there are cases which flow from rather less serious issues.

An elderly widow, Alice Frobisher, and her bachelor brother Herbert lived in a pleasant semi-detached house on the outskirts of Denley. They arrived at my office one June day in a state of considerable agitation. Alice launched straight into their complaint:

'We've got some new neighbours, Mr Francis, and their son keeps kicking a football into our garden.'

Having been guilty of this many times myself as a soccer-playing schoolboy, I already had considerable unspoken sympathy for the lad.

'We wouldn't have troubled you, Mr Francis', said Herbert, 'but yesterday evening we were out in the garden, sitting in our deck chairs, when his football landed right between us. It gave us both a nasty turn. It really is too much. Can you write to the parents to see that it doesn't happen again?'

After some discussion with them on the law of nuisance - which I explained was all a matter of degree as to whether there was any legal action they could take - I agreed to write a letter setting out my clients' complaint and seeking an assurance that there would be no repetition.

I duly wrote the letter to my clients' neighbours and after the customary preamble, in which solicitors are wont to indulge, emphasising the importance of good relations between neighbours, I pointed out that their son's behaviour in kicking a football into my clients' garden, and narrowly missing them as they sat in their deck chairs, had caused them great distress. I suggested that, to restore good neighbourly relations, he could perhaps play football somewhere else.

I hoped that my letter had combined the necessary firmness and tact, but it turned out that my mental picture of the 'offender' was somewhat amiss. The very next day a young mother marched into my office with a little boy who could not have been more than eight years old and deposited a very small rubber ball on my desk.

'Is this what your clients are complaining about, Mr Francis?', asked the young mother.

I was completely taken aback. I had had a mental picture of a rowdy teenager kicking a big leather football of the kind I used to play with as a boy - which in muddy conditions felt like a lump of concrete when it was headed. Such a ball could certainly have caused lethal damage to an old lady sitting in a deck chair. But fantasy and reality were somewhat apart.

My spontaneous laughter at the sight of the little boy and his small rubber ball seemed to take away his mother's indignation. We had a really good talk about football in general and places to play in particular. The case had a happy ending because, with the help of a local councillor whom I knew, a small field was made available for the local youngsters to use and we managed to lay on some coaching for them.

A couple of months later I was passing the field and saw some small boys playing football on it. I stopped my car and watched for a few minutes. I was pleased to see my young friend playing with great enthusiasm and really enjoying himself. At half time he came running over to me.

'This is great, Mr Francis', he said.

'I hope to see you play for England some day', I replied.

As I stood on the touchline watching the second half, I couldn't help remembering the days when I was a football-mad schoolboy myself. My football mentor was a man by the name of H E Griggs, who was a great believer in tactical team talks. So, back in the classroom after every match, the school team would gather round a large green board marked out like a football pitch. On this our football maestro would then proceed to move around brightly coloured counters at bewildering speed in a series of brilliant if highly theoretical moves. In fact, I think H E Griggs invented the deep-lying centre forward and the Revie plan before Don Revie himself did. Sadly for H E Griggs, we rarely seemed to succeed in putting his match-winning moves into practice on the actual field of play.

As I walked away from the pitch, I reflected that whether or not my young friend's tactical moves worked out or even if he played for England one day, I just hoped that he would get as much pleasure and enjoyment from the game as I had done.

The Prop Forward

I finally accepted that my serious football playing days were over a few years ago after I had taken part in a five-a-side competetion played in a local gym.

The teams were drawn from the police, magistrates' clerks, prosecuting solicitors and the local solicitors - for whom I was persuaded to turn out. If you are fit and in training, five-a-side football is a tiring game; if you are neither of these things it is positively shattering.

Towards the end of the evening, by which time I was nearly on my knees with exhaustion, I was tackled - or rather bodychecked - by a very large and powerfully-built young policeman and painfully sandwiched between him and the wall bars. Not surprisingly the police were the evening's winners, and I took three weeks to recover. I reluctantly concluded that football, particularly the five-a-side version, and squash are essentially young men's games.

The young policeman who had unknowingly brought about my retirement from football reminded me of Joe Wheelwright, a rugby league prop forward who was a client of mine and bore a striking physical resemblance to him. Joe's parents lived in Denley and had been clients of mine, so they recommended me to him.

Joe was one of my favourite clients, mainly because he gave me the excuse to talk about rugby league. I had never been keen on rugby union, partly because I had never been very good at it and partly because I always preferred playing soccer. When I wasn't playing soccer I loved watching rugby league, and of all the spectator sports I would without hesitation put rugby league at the top of my list of favourites.

I have always thought that any major sporting occasion is well worth attending, even if you are not particularly interested in the sport in question, but a rugby league cup final is undoubtedly something special. The first such final I attended was the memorable replayed final at Odsal Stadium in Bradford in 1954 when Warrington beat Halifax, and I have been privileged to watch many great matches since, as a small boy, I was part of that huge Odsal crowd.

Rugby league is very much a northern game, tough, uncompromising and totally honest. In my boyhood memories I shall forever associate it with large disciplined crowds of cloth-capped men with their scarves and rattles, the smell of old men's pipe tobacco, brass bands playing before the match and the most brilliant running and passing you will see on any pitch anywhere in the world.

If the average rugby league supporter follows his club with wit, knowledge and enthusiasm, the average rugby league player has a very disciplined approach to the game. It has never ceased to amaze me that the referees are instantly obeyed by men who are usually twice their size. It's a no-nonsense game and rugby league referees are noted for not standing any nonsense.

Like all rugby league players, Joe Wheelwright had a job in addition to playing professional rugby and his job - for which his physique made him eminently suitable - was that of a nightclub 'bouncer'. As soon as Joe knew of my interest in the game he loved to talk to me about the great players and great matches both past and present, and when we weren't talking about rugby league he regaled me with stories of his experiences at the night club. It always took me a while to get down to business with Joe, but that was as much my fault as his.

One evening Joe was being abused and taunted by a group of skinheads who were trying to get into the nightclub but he eventually persuaded them to leave. During the dispute, however, one of the youths had managed to get behind him and as Joe was watching the others leave this youth launched a ferocious kick at the back of his legs. Joe turned and instinctively threw a right-hand punch which connected with the youth's jaw and laid him unconscious at his feet. His head had hit the the concrete steps outside the club, his skull was fractured and he spent some weeks in hospital hovering between life and death before eventually recovering.

Not surprisingly, Joe had been greatly worried during this time, and his worry turned to shock and amazement when he found himself being prosecuted for assault occasioning grievous bodily harm. He asked me to defend him and to plead not guilty, relying on his contention that he had been acting in self-defence.

I had to tell him, however, that in law you are only entitled to use the minimum amount of force necessary to defend yourself, and the prosecution case would be that by knocking his assailant unconscious he had gone some way beyond that. Joe's difficulties were increased when he stood in court, because whereas he was a giant of a man his assailant was small and insignificant in appearance.

Little did the court know - as I did - that off the field at any rate Joe was a 'gentle giant', for his two abiding passions apart from rugby were his pigeon loft and his greenhouse, where he grew prize orchids. To see him gently cupping one of his racing birds in his rough hands, or to watch him carefully tending his delicate flowered orchids, was an absolute revelation.

But the members of the jury must have been excellent judges of character, for when they heard the circumstances of the incident and Joe's evidence they acquitted him of the charge after retiring for less than five minutes.

In spite of this, soon afterwards Joe retired both as a rugby league professional and as a nightclub bouncer. Like many other ex-players before him he moved away to run a pub and he stayed happily there for many years. I called in for a drink soon after he moved there, and when Joe called 'time' he did it with the same authority and immediate result as any rugby league referee ordering a player off the field for an early bath.

The Problem with Hitting Sixes

I learnt my cricket, as all Yorkshire boys surely still do, by reading of the exploits of the county's heroes - in my youth Len Hutton and Freddie Trueman were the ones to follow - and then going out into the garden or any piece of spare ground to try and emulate them.

My cricketing came in three varieties, family cricket, school cricket and club cricket. When it came to 'test matches' played with family and friends, absolutely no quarter was given and neither was there any allowance made for sex. If my sister and female cousins, who were all ferocious tacklers, held their own when we practised rugby and soccer, then bodyline bowling certainly held no terrors for them. In the manner of all brothers who secretly adore their sisters but prefer to embarrass them in public, I nicknamed my sister 'Rocky' after the world heavyweight boxing champion, Rocky Marciano. It was my brotherly way of recognising her toughness and durability in sport of any kind.

Apart from family 'test matches', we boys used to play matches in each other's gardens throughout the long summer holidays, and in these matches home advantage was all-important.

When I went to the home of my great friend Chris Hedley we played in his rather small cobbled back yard, where the danger to us through the unpredictable bounce of the 'pitch' was matched only by the danger to his mother's kitchen window, which was nicely positioned just beyond the square leg boundary. His long-suffering but splendid mother knew better than to work in the kitchen when we were playing, but she always had a bottle of pop ready for us when we had finished.

Chris's garden was on a very steep hill but he always promised a proper pitch once the garden had been levelled. Looking at its slow progress every year I always doubted it would be completed, particularly when I read in a gardening book that 'levelling should only be attempted by the amateur on a very small scale'.

So, while the pitch was always going to be ready 'next summer', I had to resign myself to heavy defeats in the back yard. In the course of one particularly long and hot summer Chris, who knew the lie of the cobbles and all their ruts and jagged edges, amassed about 5,000 runs in response to my 500. I got my revenge the following year, however, when in the return match on our tennis court - the one which doubled for cricket, football and bicycle polo and of which I knew every slope, bare patch and awkward bounce - the scores were dramatically reversed.

School cricket was equally serious in a different way and was taught to be synonymous with a moral code for life. There were hours of net and fielding practise interspersed with injunctions to 'play a straight bat' and to to 'keep your end of the wicket up'. A highlight of my schooldays was a session at the Headingley nets under the watchful eyes of the legendary Maurice Leyland.

Then there was club cricket. In Yorkshire this falls into two categories, league and village. League cricket in Yorkshire is deadly serious, competitive and an ideal preparation for county players. Village cricket is rather less serious and it was this sort that always appealed to me. For some years whilst still at school I was an honorary member of the local village team. We played our home games on a pitch cut out of the middle of a hayfield, and if the pitch was improvised so was the team. But we enjoyed every minute of it!

A club not unlike the one I played for was Nether Heylands, a village not too far away from Denley. For as long as anyone could remember, Nether Heylands had played its cricket matches in a field which it rented from a farmer. One day the neighbouring farmer obtained planning permission for four bungalows to be built on one of his fields adjoining the cricket ground, and it was then that the club's problems began.

The main problem was that any balls hit for six over the square leg boundary were likely to land in the bungalows' gardens, and sometimes broke windows in greenhouses, conservatories and even the bungalows themselves. The club did its best to resolve the problem by putting up extra wire netting and changing the position of the pitch, but there was absolutely nothing that could be done to prevent a big hit going clean out of the ground and into someone's garden.

Three of the bungalow owners adopted an understanding and conciliatory attitude towards the problem. They realised that the club had been there many years before they came, and didn't mind too much if a few cricket balls landed in their garden from time to time.

The fourth bungalow owners, however, adopted a different attitude altogether. Harry and Jean Brown had moved to the country from the suburbs, and you could tell that by looking at the bungalow and its immaculate garden with its manicured lawn, chiming door bells and gnomes fishing in a little goldfish pond. Harry was a self-made Yorkshire businessman, the new bungalow was his pride and joy and when cricket balls landed in his garden - and even worse when there was broken glass - he reacted angrily and uncompromisingly.

The club paid for the damage and the cost of any repairs, but the Browns were not to be so easily appeased. They consulted solicitors who in turn wrote to the club secretary threatening legal action unless the nuisance ceased. The club committee asked me to advise them and instructed me to defend any action brought. They really had no choice, as the very future of the club was at stake.

The meeting with the committee drew to a close, with the members filled with dismay at the prospect of litigation and possible closure. I suddenly had a thought:

'Do you know if the Browns have a son?', I asked the secretary.

'No', he replied, 'why?'

He raised his voice above the general talking and called out across the room:

'Does anyone know if the Browns have a son?'

'Yes', shouted back one of the members, 'they've a lad about fifteen called Ben. But who wants to know?'

'I was just wondering', I replied quietly, 'if he plays cricket.'

Following the meeting I made some enquiries, found out which school young Ben attended and had a word with the sports master there, Dave Simpson, who by a happy chance was a friend of mine.

'Can Ben play cricket?', I asked.

'Can he play?', Dave exclaimed, 'I'll say he can play! I reckon he's the most promising cricketer for his age I've ever seen at this school.'

'Do his parents know?'

'Well it's funny you should ask that John, because I don't think they do. When they come to school, all they seem to be interested in is his work.'

'In that case, I think it's time they did know', I said. 'But first of all I'd like to see young Ben down at the nets on the next club practice night.'

Well Dave certainly wasn't lying! Obviously Ben wanted to emulate the great Yorkshire heroes a little more keenly than most other young lads, for he came through his trial in the nets with flying colours and was selected on merit to play for Nether Heylands the following Saturday afternoon - at home to their deadliest rivals Upper Heylands. I went along to watch and was encouraged when I spotted Ben's parents among the small group of spectators standing alongside me behind the boundary ropes.

Upper Heylands batted first and were all out for 150. This should have been quite beatable, but Nether Heylands' batting collapsed and they had only managed fifty runs for the loss of six wickets when Ben came to the crease. The club captain who had opened the batting was still there and Ben, playing like a seasoned regular, sensibly concentrated on defence whilst his captain did all the scoring. He and Ben stopped the rot, and soon the runs started to flow.

Some of the more knowledgeable ones in the crowd were soon remarking that they had 'nivver seen a lad bat wi' such a cool head on 'is young shoulders'.

Up went the 100 and then came the 125 on the scoreboard. The excitement grew. But Ben and his captain were running out of overs fast, and when the last over of the match began Nether Heylands were still twelve runs short of victory. Off the first five balls they managed to scramble six runs, which meant that a six was needed from the last ball. Ben took strike, the bowler decided to play safe by delivering what he thought would be an unplayable bouncer down the leg side but in the tension of the moment he became over-anxious and didn't pitch the ball short enough or bowl it fast enough. Ben

saw it coming all the way and with perfect timing he struck a magnificent hook shot which sent the ball soaring into the air.

'It's going to be a six alright', I thought as I watched it fly majestically over my head, 'but look where it's going to land.'

The next thing we heard was the loud shattering of glass as the ball went straight through Harry Brown's prized picture window. As the clapping and cheering at a famous victory died down, I heard the club captain telling Ben that if he carried on like this he'd be sure to play for Yorkshire some day. Then I heard the club secretary looking nervous as he talked to Ben's parents and offered to pay for the damage.

'Oh bugger t' window', said Ben's father. 'What about that though, eh? T' lad gave it some wood, didn't he?', he added with obvious pride.

After that Ben played regularly for the club and, though he never did play for the county, whenever and wherever he played his parents were always there to watch him.

Gone Fishing

Sporting life in the country is by no means restricted to bat, ball and racquet games. Hunting, shooting and fishing are the traditional country sports of rural England, and I once had a client who pursued all three with equal enthusiasm.

Henry Belford had inherited from his parents a small estate and a woollen mill. He was no businessman, however, and it wasn't long before he had to close the mill. He remained in business in a small way by acting as a middle man in the buying and selling of yarn. This left him free to concentrate on the running of his estate and to pursue his hunting, shooting and fishing.

He engaged me to do all his business legal work but he was surely one of the most frustrating clients I have ever had. More often than not there was no reply when I phoned him, and when I went round to his office there would be a sign hung up on the door saying 'Gone fishing', 'Gone shooting' or 'Gone hunting'.

To my mind, Henry should never have been in business at all because his heart simply wasn't in it. Indeed I could never get him to talk business for very long before he would change the subject and regale me animatedly with tales of his last fishing trip, shooting party or day's hunting. He was drawn as if by a magnet to the trout stream, to the red grouse on the purple moors and to the music of the hounds in full cry. He had never married and as his needs were small he felt free to go when and where he pleased.

Henry only really liked two kinds of shooting, namely grouse shooting and rough shooting, because he reckoned shooting was for sport and for the pot. He had no time for organised syndicate shoots of reared birds which, he would remark, had to be virtually kicked into the air before they were shot. He didn't regard that as any kind of sport at all.

In his younger days Henry had ridden enthusiastically to foxhounds and waded in rivers with the blue and scarlet-clad otter hunters, but now that he was older he found following the beagles more congenial. He knew the surrounding countryside so well that without expending too much effort he was able to make for a vantage point from which he could see the hounds working. A day with the beagles always seemed to finish very conveniently near to a pub, which suited Henry just fine for he also liked a drink.

I think, however, that fishing was Henry's favourite sport. When I talked to him -as often I did - about fishing, his magnificent white handlebar moustache would twitch and a schoolboy gleam would come into his eyes as he relished the prospect of a mayfly hatch or a salmon-fishing trip to Scotland.

But although greatly skilled with the rod, Henry was no dry fly purist. In fact there was nothing he liked better than a spot of upstream worming for trout, and when the trout season ended he switched to grayling, a fish which for some reason is looked down upon in the south but quite rightly is highly regarded by northern fishermen.

Nor were Henry's fishing interests confined to game fish, for he occasionally invited me to fish the private lake on his estate, and we caught some fine carp there using pieces of potato as bait.

As the years went by Henry neglected his business more and more. His financial postion steadily worsened and he took longer to pay his bills. But if he didn't give me money when I went to see him, I could be sure of coming away with a brace of grouse, a trout or a fine-looking salmon for my table. It all had to end of course, because the business was going downhill rapidly and the estate - which had been mainly kept going to serve his sporting interests - was also losing money.

One lovely summer afternoon Henry phoned and asked me to come to his office. As I went in I saw his accountant standing grave-faced next to him. The crunch had finally come, the business was insolvent and Henry's beloved estate would have to be sold. After we had talked for a little while it was clear that nothing could be done to save the situation. Henry stood up and said:

'Well, gentlemen, you'll have to excuse me now, I'm going fishing.'

'That's been his trouble all along', remarked the accountant to me after he had gone.

Henry didn't make for the carp lake on his estate but for his own private paradise, a former monastery fish pond in the heart of the Denley woods to which he had exclusive fishing rights. He had lovingly restored the pond and stocked it carefully with brown and rainbow trout. Here and only here he insisted on the fly. It was in this sylvan paradise, in the warm sunshine of a summer evening, that he collapsed and died whilst casting his last fly. Henry had finally 'gone fishing'.

Clients, Characters and Friends

Clients

Like the rest of the human race, most clients are delightful, sensible people who are a pleasure to represent, and nobody ever made a good solicitor who did not enjoy meeting people and trying to help them with their problems.

Years ago most of the population had little or no contact with lawyers. Their principal function was to look after the interests of the privileged minority who had land and money, whilst the poor were represented by the profession merely as an act of charity. Nowadays, with the spread of home ownership and the provision of legal aid, the solicitor in general practice sees a very wide range of clients from all walks of life and he soon becomes familiar with the different types of client.

There is the would-be businessman who is always having bright ideas which never work; there is the downtrodden wife whose statement you are about to take will predictably consist of a catalogue of beatings, drunkenness, abuse and infidelity by her husband; and then there is the married couple. I always know when a couple have been married for some years by the way they constantly interrupt each other, finish each other's sentences and fill in each other's memory gaps. Not so long ago I had in my office a grand old Dales couple who were trying to give me their side of the story, but they both had different stories!

'Well, Mr Francis', the wife began, 'it were like this yer see. T' trouble 'appened last Tuesday ∸

'Nay lass, tha's gone an' gitten it all wrong', interrupted the husband with what he thought was the voice of authority. 'Mr Francis, Wednesday last it was ∸

'There you go again', she retorted. 'Now just let me tell the gentleman the tale.'

'Nay woman, story's got to be told reet. You'll 'ave to excuse t' missus, Mr Francis, 'er mind's not what it were thirty year sin, nivver mind last week. Now it were Wednesday when t' police stopped us when we were goin' ovver Black Knot Pass ∸

The wife shook her head. 'Through t' top o' Grassdale', she muttered just loud enough for her husband to hear.

By listening to both sides of what seemed to be a never-ending tale I managed to piece together what had happened. Interviews of this type tend to take rather a long time.

Then again there are the clients who are not over-bright. With such clients I have found that no matter how detailed are the instructions given to them, they will still contrive to get them wrong. If, for instance, they are asked to sign a document 'where indicated in pencil' it will almost certainly be returned signed in pencil, and if they are asked to have their signatures on a document witnessed by two independent persons they will, as likely as not, come back witnessed by relatives - and with the signatures in the wrong place.

Then there are the cheeky 'clients', the kind of people who come into the office to ask if we supply will forms - free of course. Only the other week a lady came into our office and asked if she could use our telephone as a matter of urgency.

May I ask why?', I enquired.

'I'm sure you won't mind', she replied, 'it's just that I need to speak to my own solicitor urgently.'

There are times when, believe it or not, even a lawyer is lost for words.

But the client I most dread seeing is the one who comes in accompanied by a 'friend', and it is this 'friend' who does all the talking. To try and converse with the client in such a situation is like trying to talk to a ventriloquist's dummy!

Then again there is the occasional drunken client who always telephones from a police station at three o'clock in the morning. I have always thought that a solicitor's ability and indeed his inclination to assist in such circumstances is rather limited, for the combination of a half-asleep laywer and a drunken client is unlikely to be a productive one.

'I'll see you in the morning when I'm awake and you're sober', is about the best advice I can usually offer.

There is, unfortunately, a residual but ever-present minority of clients who by one means or another contrive to make their solicitor's life a merry hell. They are the clients who telephone at least twice a day every day to enquire as to the progress of their case, who insist on an immediate appointment then fail to keep it or who decide to go on holiday in the middle of important transactions. Only last summer I had to make telephone calls to the Algarve, a Greek island and a remote part of North Wales in a desperate attempt to contact holidaying couples whose conveyancing transactions had reached the critical stage.

The problems presented by difficult clients may be different, but they all have one feature in common which is, when anything goes wrong they invariably blame their solicitor. There is something else I have noticed too. Those clients for whom you have sweated blood and who have been most demanding in terms of time and attention never, but never, express any gratitude. This is far more likely to come from a client for whom some trifling service has been performed.

Every solicitor must find his own way of dealing with difficult clients. I was once advised by a very wise and experienced practitioner that a solicitor should in no circumstances lose his temper with a client, for such behaviour was inappropriate for a professional man who should be able to exercise self-control at all times. I am quite sure the advice is sound although it cannot be the easiest to follow throughout a lifetime of practice.

Some clients continually do those things they ought not to do and leave undone those things they ought to do. Several winters ago there was a particularly bitterly cold and snowy January day when just myself and my secretary managed to make it to the office.

Only one client braved the atrocious conditions to visit the office during the whole day. My secretary and I both thought it must be a matter of extreme urgency as we helped him off with his coat and hat, reviving him with a cup of tea liberally laced with whisky.

It turned out, however, that he was a farmer who had walked several miles over the hills to call and sign his will that had been typed and waiting for him since the previous June! He had obviously just got it into his head to come in and sign it, and that is just what he did do. 'There's nowt so queer as folks', I reflected as I watched him disappear back into the blizzard outside.

I have often thought that a solicitor dealing with clients is rather like an actor being on centre stage with various characters joining him there from time to time. Some will occupy the stage for longer than others, some will disappear quickly and others will reappear from time to time. The solicitor knows better than most that everyone has his or her problems, and that every client has a story to tell. He knows, too, that truth is indeed very often much stranger than fiction, and some of my own client 'characters' and their stories bear eloquent testimony to this fact.

The Colonel's Story

'Colonel Horrocks to see you, Mr Francis', said my receptionist on the office intercom.

'Ask him to come straight in', I replied.

I sat back in my chair not knowing quite what to expect. The only background information I had was a note from the colonel's telephone message that he urgently wanted my advice 'on his (query) matrimonial position'. I could not begin to speculate on what the 'query' might be, so all I could do was to sit back and listen to his story.

Colonel Sebastian Horrocks DSO MC was now an old man, although you could tell just by looking at him that he was still a typical soldier in appearance and had led a full, varied and interesting life.

For a start he had gone through the two world wars and had been decorated for bravery in both. Inbetween, and afterwards, he had worked in the colonies, had been a travel correspondent, a dog trainer, a poultry farmer and the proprietor of several hotels.

But there had also been girls, debt and bankruptcy and latterly his life had become clouded by ill-health. Now he had very little money left, his health was failing fast and he had been warned by his doctor that he was unlikely to live for more than a few months. I did not interrupt him as he told me the story of his life - at much greater length than I have done - and waited patiently for him to come to the point of our meeting.

'Six months ago, Francis, I did the best thing I have ever done in life. I married Mary. We'd been together for about five years and I thought it was about time I did something about it. Trouble is, I reckon I've probably committed bigamy at least once and it's all going to come out when I die.'

'Bigamy? More than once?', I repeated.

I could see that my look of surprise worried him.

'Well, even if you have', I hurriedly went on to say, 'it's not a hanging offence these days. But please explain to me exactly why you think you're a bigamist'.

'Happened this way, Francis. When I was a young man I was a bit wild and got myself

75

something of a reputation with the ladies. Just before I went off to fight in the fourteen-eighteen war I got a barmaid called Suzy into trouble. Father threatened to disown me, then wanted to pay her off but in the stubborness of youth I decided to marry the girl instead. Absolutely hopeless from the start of course, never stood a chance of working, different types and all that. She wanted to be out drinking and dancing and having a good time. Couldn't keep up with her and didn't want to. Anyway the war started, off I went and I never heard from Suzy again. Did hear from friends that she lost the baby and had taken up with another fella but it was wartime and news was difficult to come by.

After the war was over, I did ask around a bit but couldn't find out where she was living or what had become of her. Three years later I met another girl called Rachel and after a very short acquaintance she persuaded me against my better judgement to marry her. We went through a civil ceremony at the registry office. I never told her about Suzy or my earlier marriage. As far as I knew both mother and child were still in existence.

Marriage to Rachel was a disaster from the word go. She wanted to be with her mother all the time, particularly after her father died. Never could stand Rachel's mother and it got so that we couldn't be in the same room together. Well, Francis, it came to the point that I told Rachel she'd jolly well have to choose between her mother and me. She chose her mother and just walked out on me one day. We hadn't been married a year when it happened. Haven't seen or heard from her since that day and frankly, Francis, haven't wanted to either.

Lot of water under the bridge since then. Jolly careful where women were concerned until five years ago I met Mary and six months ago we got married. Made rather a mess of things with women all my life. Can't believe I've found happiness, Francis, and where Mary's concerned it's true. Trouble is I've never told her the truth about my past and I'm as worried as hell about it. Haven't long to go now and the truth may come out when I'm gone. Have I committed bigamy or rather, have I committed bigamy twice? Couldn't stand hurting the old girl if she finds out the truth about me.'

'We don't know what the truth is, colonel, and that's what we've got to find out', I said quietly.

I then took down as many details of names, dates and places as the colonel could give me and asked him to leave his problem with me whilst I made some enquiries.

On the face of it I had taken on a rather daunting task but fortunately England must still be one of the best countries in the world for keeping records of births, marriages, deaths and divorces. Thank goodness for Somerset House, parish registers and county court records. Within several weeks I had completed my enquiries and asked the colonel to call in to see me again. I came straight to the point.

'Well, colonel, I'm delighted to be able to put your mind at rest. I've got documentary evidence here to prove that Suzy died before you married Rachel, and Rachel obtained a legal divorce from you before you married Mary. You haven't committed bigamy once, twice or at all, and you and Mary are legally married.'

The Colonel had been very lucky, I thought, but I reckoned he deserved a little happiness and peace of mind before he died.

The Colonel now smiled for the first time as an expression of sheer relief crossed his face, and the burden of age and worry was visibly lifted from his shoulders as he thanked me and left the office.

It was some little time before I heard from the colonel again. It was in the form of a postcard. After he had taken Mary on a round-the-world cruise, they had retired to a small cottage on an estate in the West Country which the colonel described as 'just the ticket'. He had found contentment and heartsease at last.

Father Tom

I have already told of the influence upon me of two parsons who were not my clients. There was however another parson who was my client and whose visits to the office could be guaranteed to distract me from the business in hand albeit in a totally predictable way.

The Reverend Thomas Algernon Fortescue-Brown was a High Church priest of the old school. He possessed a most beautiful clerical speaking voice, and his Sunday Mass and evening services were most impressive until the moment came for him to ascend the pulpit and preach. For he was an eccentric and forgetful man and his sermons were liable to be on any subject under the sun - from the state of the church boiler to his travel experiences in Outer Mongolia. He always started with a text, but by no means confined himself to it. Indeed he seldom came back to it.

The older he got the more eccentric, forgetful and repetitive he became. He eventually reached the stage that it didn't really matter what he said because his parishioners had come to accept him for what he was, one of their village characters.

'Father Tom', as he was affectionately known in his parish, used to call in to see me at my office from time to time, but when he came he had generally completely forgotten the reason for his visit so he told me stories instead.

Normally I am quite happy to sit back and listen to a good yarn but the trouble with Father Tom's stories was that they were always the same yarns. One, probably his favourite, concerned his adventures long ago as the skipper of an Icelandic trawler when the vessel had gone down in a storm; another was a tale about his days as a missionary bringing the word of God to a savage tribe in West Africa; and the third was about the time he had played centre-half when only seventeen for Arsenal in an exciting cup tie.

At first I was impressed - if a little sceptical - but fairly soon after Father Tom became my client I discovered that I was by no means the only one selected to hear those stories. I also found it to be common knowledge in his parish that their priest had never been an Icelandic trawler skipper nor an African missionary, still less had he played centre-half or indeed any other position for Arsenal. I think he had told the stories so often over so many years to so many people that he now genuinely believed them to be true.

Father Tom was such a delightful man, however, that nobody, least of all myself, had the heart to question the truthfulness of his recounted exploits. But after I had heard all three stories (which, incidentally, never seemed to come to an end) a number of times

I developed a ploy for bringing the appointment to a conclusion. There was, after all, other work to be done.

I arranged with my secretary before each appointment that she would allow me no more than ten minutes to conduct my necessary business and she would then buzz me on the office intercom. If at that point Father Tom was just launching himself into one of his stories, I could tell him that he would have to excuse me as I had to dash out of the office on an emergency case.

So I never did hear what finally happened when a crowd of hostile natives were surrounding his missionary hut, how his Icelandic trawler survived in mountainous seas or whether Arsenal managed to hold on to a one goal lead when they were down to eight men and Father Tom was all that stood between them and defeat.

'I'm sorry, John', he would say with exquisite courtesy, 'I'm taking up too much of your time. You must go straight away but never mind, dear boy, I'll tell you the rest of the story next time.'

Father Tom was the bane of his bishop's life, not just because his eccentricity and forgetfulness brought complaints from his parishioners from time to time but mainly because he had a total aversion to filling in forms of any kind. When I used to call to see him at the vicarage there were always piles of unopened letters, forms and questionnaires lying around in his study from the diocese to which he had made no attempt whatever to reply.

'Just forms, dear boy', he would say to me when he saw me looking at them.

But if he exasperated the church bureaucracy, he was loved by all the failures, problem families and hopeless cases in the parish, with whom he spent much of his time. Some of these cases he referred to me when legal advice was necessary, but Father Tom maintained his interest in them even when in one or two cases the client he had referred to me ended up in prison.

He would go on regular prison visits and I used to smile slightly at the picture of Father Tom holding court in the company of a captive audience of prisoners and regaling them with his favourite stories which I had heard so often, stories which he started but which, unlike Magnus Magnusson in *Mastermind*, he never finished.

From Out of the Mouths of Babes and Sucklings

One of my family friends who lived in the same parish as Father Tom told me of a time he fell prey to the priest's forgetfulness. Peter, his wife and their two small children were going away on holiday for a fortnight and Father Tom had asked them if he could leave his car in their drive whilst his own garage was being repaired.

Now Peter, who knew the priest's reputation only too well, hesitated for a moment, for he had the feeling that something would go wrong, but he smiled his agreement to the request which in all Christian charity he didn't feel able to refuse. He did stipulate, however, that the car should be removed by the Sunday following his return, as on that day he and his family were to go to a hotel for a lunch party to celebrate his parents' wedding anniversary.

Peter and his family came back from holiday and the first thing they noticed was that Father Tom's old car was still parked in their drive, so much to his annoyance Peter had to park his car on the main road. Sunday morning came and Father Tom's car was still there.

'Well, thank goodness he's not blocking our way out', said Peter to his wife. 'We'll get off to the hotel now and I'll ring the vicar later and ask him to shift it.'

Peter's parents were noted for two things where family gatherings were concerned: the first was that they expected their relatives, particularly their younger relatives, to dress up for the occasion; and secondly and most importantly they expected them to be punctual. By the time Peter and his wife and children were dressed and ready to go they were already a few minutes late.

'Come on, let's get off, or you know what father will say', shouted Peter as his wife came down the drive with the children to join him in the car.

It was at this moment that Father Tom arrived to collect his car. All would have been well and Peter would still have got off if one of his children hadn't decided to go to the toilet, and whilst little Johnny was in the toilet Father Tom was trying, with an obvious lack of success, to start his car.

'Could you come and take a look at it for me, dear boy,' he called to Peter.

With a frozen smile, Peter got out of his car, trudged up the drive and lifted up the bonnet of Father Tom's old Ford. After fiddling with the carburettor and getting his hands very greasy in the process, he decided there was nothing obviously wrong and reckoned the best thing to do was to give the priest's car a push start. With his wife's help, and after three unsuccessful attempts, Father Tom's car eventually started and he drove away down the road, giving a cheery wave to the dishevelled family standing behind him.

By this time Peter was absolutely speechless. He was hot, he was angry, he was late and he would have to wash again and put on another suit. When he eventually set off in the car he turned to his wife and exclaimed, perhaps rather moderately in the circumstances, 'That bloody vicar!'

About two weeks later Peter and his wife were walking in the village with their children when who should they meet but Father Tom. As the priest came right up to them he smiled his benign and heavenly smile, but it was little Johnny who spoke first.

'Look, daddy, it's that bloody vicar,' he said.

'All of them?'

A very different type of client to Father Tom was Commander George Richard Murrie (Royal Navy, retired). Whereas Father Tom was assuredly not for this earthly life, the commander was in every sense a man of the world. His booming, cheerful voice which heralded his arrival at our reception desk could be heard right down the corridor, and although his problems - both legal and non-legal - were many and various I was always glad to see him.

If George Richard Murrie had not had a girl in every port, then he very nearly had. He had an eye for the ladies, and his eye was keen. But at the age of seventy he had met a widow whom he wished to marry. The problem was that he still had a wife who preferred to play the 'injured innocent' rather than agree to a divorce, even though the marriage had been an empty shell for years and they had lived apart for some time.

Eventually however, and after considering a very generous financial provision she indicated that she would not contest a petition and I made an appointment to see the commander with a view to setting divorce proceedings in motion. When he came in, I had to keep him waiting for a few minutes whilst I attended to another client.

Sitting in the waiting room with him happened to be a female client waiting to see one of my partners also about a divorce. This good lady who, I learnt later, was living in shocking accomodation and some poverty, proceeded to tell the commander her entire life history, by no means sparing him the intimate details of the sexual problems in her marriage.

I think my good friend the commander was rather flattered if somewhat surprised to be taken into her confidence, but as I observed to him later I have not found it unusual for a client - particularly one in divorce proceedings - to open up much more to our receptionist or secretary or indeed another client than to a solicitor!

Eventually when the commander eventually excused himself and came into my office he said, 'Well, Francis, I've just been talking to one of your clients and I really wonder whether I've got any problems at all.'

I understood exactly what he meant. For I have always thought that there is nothing like a client's problems for putting your own in perspective, and there is nothing like being a solicitor for being constantly reminded of the old adage that there is always somebody worse off than yourself.

'Anyway, Francis, about my divorce', went on the commander, suddenly bringing our philosophical discussion to an end. 'What can you do for me?'

Now at the time this discussion took place - which was some years ago - the divorce laws had not been liberalised as much as they are now. The main grounds were cruelty, adultery and desertion. None of them fitted the bill. His wife had not been cruel, she had certainly not committed adultery and a petition based on desertion looked difficult to say the least. However they had been apart for the past five years and she had told him to leave, so I thought we might just get a petition on its feet.

'It's constructive desertion or nothing', I told him.

But there was at least one other formidable obstacle in the way of a successful suit. In those days any person petitioning for divorce had to make a statement saying whether he or she had committed adultery and if so to provide full details and ask the court to exercise its discretion in respect of it. This was as often as not a singularly embarrassing procedure both for the solicitor and client, particularly if the client happened to be a friend as well.

'Sorry, commander, but I'm obliged to ask you this. I need details of anyone, if at all, with whom you have had sexual intercourse other than your wife since you were married.'

A smile crossed the commander's face and there was a twinkle in his eye as he replied, 'What? Good God, man! All of them?'

I seem to remember that it took several sheets of paper to contain his list which was submitted 'for the exercise of the court's discretion'. No doubt it made fascinating reading! The judge appeared to wince slightly when they were handed to him, and I was as relieved as my client when he decided to 'exercise the court's discretion' and to grant his divorce.

Madame Josephine

Another client of mine who was a familiar sight in Denley was Madame Josephine Defêvre. She was a cultured lady, distantly descended from a French aristocratic family. In her younger days she had been a teacher and I used to go to her cottage as a schoolboy for extra French tuition. These extra lessons were better than school because she really made me think as well as speak the language, and taught me to use certain French expressions nearly every day of my life.

Even though I have made no serious attempt to speak the language for years, expressions like c'est la vie, je ne sais quoi, joie de vivre, savoir faire, revenons à ces moutons, cherchez la femme, pour encourager les autres and bon chance still figure in my conversation.

When I first knew her Madame Josephine was a very plump, bosomy woman. In fact when I was in my teens she had a bigger bosom than any other woman I knew - with the solitary exception of my ballroom dancing teacher, Miss Prendergast. Now she really had an enormous bosom, and if I had ever been asked by Wilfred Pickles on his radio programme *Have a Go* to describe my most embarrassing moment I would without hesitation have recalled the occasion when she picked me out of her class to join her in a demonstration foxtrot.

'Now come on, John, get hold of me properly', she called out in her stentorian tones as she squeezed and crushed me within her hold.

Oh, the agony and despair of adolescence when all the most desirable women seem hopelessly unattainable and the least desirable are the most pressing in their attention!

Madame Josephine had been married briefly but her husband had died. As she became older, the more eccentric and the lonelier she become and she gradually outlived all her friends. When she had first come to live in Denley she had been none too popular, particularly with tradesman calling with deliveries to her front door. 'Round the back', she would say to them with a majestic wave of her hand. They called her 'Lady Muck', but as she grew older and lonelier and they realised her manner was inbuilt rather than deliberate, their attitude towards her changed and she became known affectionately as 'Josie' by everyone in the town.

By the time I had qualified and had acquired her as a client, Josie's appearance had changed out of all recognition and her plump bosomy figure had been reduced to a bent, shrivelled and painfully thin old lady. She had become a virtual recluse and because I was one of her few points of contact with the outside world she was forever haunting my office. She was prone to change her will every few weeks, to claim damages every time she tripped on a pavement, to change her investments on a whim or simply to call in for a chat.

One day she telephoned and summoned me to attend her at her cottage. When I got there I found the back door open and Josie called to me to go up to her bedroom. She was ill and lying in bed propped up by pillows.

'Do I know you very well, John?', she asked me.

This was a leading question if ever I had heard one. But before I could answer she went on 'There's a chamber pot under my bed which is rather full, could you empty it for me?'

'They never told me about this at law school,' I thought as I complied with her request.

I realised afterwards that I had made a mistake in emptying that chamber pot because from then on Josie was liable to phone me at any time of the day or night if anything untoward had happened to her.

Josie had two main weaknesses. The first was for cats, of which there seemed to be an inordinate number in her cottage. The second was for alcohol. She was prone from time to time to break her isolation by going to pubs on her own and drinking much more than was good for her.

One evening I had just gone to bed when the telephone rang. It was Josie and she sounded pretty hysterical and rather the worse for drink.

'John, John', she cried, 'something absolutely ghastly has happened.' She then started screaming incoherently and then broke down completely.

'Calm down, Josie, take your time and tell me the problem,' I said as sympathetically as I could.

'John, John, you know I've got a glass eye, don't you? Well I've just got home from the pub and I've swallowed it by mistake in a glass of water. Oh dear, oh my God, I'm going to die.'

Her voice tailed off and she started crying hysterically again.

'Have you phoned your doctor?' I asked.

'Not yet,' she replied, 'I wanted to tell you first. Will you phone the doctor for me, John . . . please?'

The things a solicitor has to do, I thought, as I told Josie to stay in bed whilst I arranged for her doctor to come and see her.

Doctor James Meredith was an experienced and very good general practitioner, but not noted for having great sympathy with his patients. When I telephoned him late at night and told him of Josie's problem, he was certainly none too enthusiastic at the prospect of going to see her. The next day, however, when I chanced to meet him in town I found that he had recovered his sense of humour.

'Did you manage to deal with Josie's problem?' I asked.

'I hope so', he replied with a grin, 'I told her to go to sleep and keep a steady look out for it in the morning - with her other eye!'

The Headmaster

I was always particularly pleased to see Geoffrey Woodhead. He had retired to his native Yorkshire after a lifetime of teaching in different schools around the country. His had been a career which was rounded off by the successful headmastership of a large state school in the Midlands.

As a general rule, solicitors consider teachers and lecturers to be among their most difficult clients - a little learning being a dangerous thing and all that - but Geoffrey was an exception because he was a friend more than a client.

He shared with me a love of books, poetry, literature, wine and amateur dramatics. It was, in fact, at our local dramatic society where we had first met and as we fell into conversation I recognised in him a kindred spirit. Although an accomplished actor Geoffrey preferred to produce plays, and we amateurs were lucky indeed to have such a wise and experienced producer. His long life as a teacher enabled him both to maintain discipline and impart knowledge, and his wide reading and love of literature gave him a remarkable insight into character, an understanding of what a play was about and a real feel for theatre.

I have always thought that the best part of being in a play is the rehearsals, for if by learning together and laughing together the members of the cast build up a good rapport and team spirit, they are the better prepared for whatever may go wrong on the night.

Geoffrey, who had produced more plays than he cared to remember, knew very well that however good the preparation and rehearsals had been, or for that matter however bad thay had been, it was not inevitable that the play would be 'alright on the night', as actors are forever saying to each other. But he was always philosophical at times of crisis or when things went awry.

So he grinned with me when, at the very start of one play a group of pensioners, who had come in at half price on the first night, whispered loudly on my first entrance 'That's John Francis, isn't it?' He laughed with me over my mistakes, like the time I said to my leading lady, 'I didn't want our love to be secret and fertile', when the last word should have been 'furtive'. He suffered with me when the audience waited in silence for what seemed an eternity for me to open a champagne bottle on stage which stubbornly refused to open, and joined in the cheers with the audience when it finally did. And he felt for the whole cast in another play when the leading man, who was meant casually to open a French window and stroll into the drawing room from the garden, found that it had inadvertently been fastened from the inside. The whole cast waited silent and helpless as he shook the window a number of times, then finally had to resort to putting his hand through what was meant to be a glass window in order to make his entrance.

Sometimes we would rehearse for plays at Geoffrey's house, and after the rest of the cast had gone home, we would sit together long into the night talking of books, poetry, literature and plays, swapping quotations and comparing the merits of our favourite authors. As we talked, and he was expounding the merits of Milton and I was defending Wordsworth and he was telling me why he was a Dornford Yates man and I was explaining why I preferred John Buchan, our tongues were well and truly loosened by Geoffrey's liberally-supplied drinks - for he was a great enthusiast for home-made wines and beers, all without exception both very drinkable and highly potent.

As the drinks flowed and our conversation moved from the subject of books and literature to philosophy and life in general, Geoffrey would usually come out with one of his favourite sayings - after making sure that his wife was well out of earshot!:

'The man that loveth wine, hath his senses sometimes, the man that loveth women never.'

Away from amateur dramatics, Geoffrey, like me, continually haunted secondhand bookshops, attended book fairs and went to jumble sales on the chance of picking up some valuable first edition for a few pence. Over the years he accumulated a splendid library of over four thousand books until there were books all over the house and his long-suffering wife finally put her foot down. 'I have to smuggle them in now', he told me on one of his last visits to the office.

Geoffrey had tried during his many years as a teacher with varying degrees of success to communicate his love of books to his pupils. Most of them, however, seemed to prefer watching television. This concerned him greatly, not because he objected to television as such but because he insisted it could be no substitute for reading, which he felt would open their minds and imagination in a way which television could never do.

Geoffrey's library was the envy of his bookloving friends, and a number of local dealers were known to be licking their lips at the prospect of their eventual disposal. They did not know what I knew, however, for I had prepared his will, and when he died its provision concerning his library came as both a surprise and a shock to the people of Denley. For he had directed his executors to arrange an open day to enable all the local schoolchildren to choose for themselves any books they wanted from his library, and absolutely free.

The dealers could only look on in frustration as a steady stream of pupils past and present filed into the hall we had hired to choose their books. What a lucky dip it was, for most of them did not have a clue whether they were taking away a good read worth a few pence or a valuable first edition worth hundreds of pounds. What a splendid and generous idea this was I thought as the last of the books was carried away. Geoffrey's widow was pleased too.

'At long last I'll be able to move about in my own house', she said.

Pitch and Putt

Children of my generation all had lots of 'aunties'. This was because we not only had relatives who were real aunties but because in those days we would call all our female family friends and neighbours 'auntie' too. Some of those who were not real aunties greatly enriched our lives and were very special indeed.

There were in my boyhood three such aunties who stand out in my memory. The first of these was Auntie Flo. She was a smiling and generous old lady, the type of auntie to brighten any child's day by saying 'here's a little something for you' as she patted small fingers which she had just closed over a ten shilling note. She was also rather bent, stooping and exceptionally small, so small that when she drove her car she looked through the steering wheel rather than over it. But it was not so much her somewhat hair-raising driving for which I remember her but rather for her visits to our Sunday afternoon tea parties.

Nobody bothers to make afternoon tea any more, or so I thought until quite recently when an elderly client of mine asked me to call in on him for a cup of tea and to discuss making a new will.

When I duly arrived at his cottage I found to my surprise and delight that a proper afternoon tea had been laid on by his wife in honour of my visit. There on a table covered by a beautiful white table cloth was her best china, silver tea service and all the accompanying ingredients of a proper old-fashioned English afternoon tea. First there were the neatly cut sandwiches of several varieties, including cucumber of course, there was a home-made date and walnut cake and finally a wealth of so many other different cakes, sweets and delicacies that after I had got through a creditable selection of them, I could only rise from my chair with difficulty. I turned to my hosts to thank them.

'Just a cup of tea, you said.'

'Well', replied my client, 'we don't get many visitors these days, so we like to make the most of them.'

This totally unexpected tea party had taken my mind back to Auntie Flo and to the marvellous afternoon tea parties of my childhood when assorted relatives came together at our home on a Sunday afternoon. We children used to make pigs of ourselves on these occasions quite shamelessly. It was my cousin David who held the record for pancakes - one afternoon he ate thirteen.

Talking of thirteen brings me straight back to Auntie Flo, because the only problem I ever remember with our afternoon teas was that through some twist of fate there were generally thirteen of us. Auntie Flo, who was highly superstitious, objected to thirteen sitting at a table together. This meant that out of respect for her wishes two of us had to sit at a separate small table, and this invariably caused arguments as to which of us children would be the volunteers. Looking back, it is no wonder we used up so much energy in the games we all played - we needed to after those teas.

The second aunt to stand out in my memory was an infant school teacher in a nearby village who was known by all the children in the district as Auntie Jane. I was one of the many local children who knew and loved her and I will always associate her in my mind with flowers and picnics. When I was very young, Auntie Jane was responsible for starting my education in botany, an education which was continued by my Scottish granny whose knowledge of, and green fingers with, rock plants of every description was quite exceptional.

85

I remember Auntie Jane as a cheerful, jolly person who adored children and who possessed an infectious enthusiasm for all of nature's wonders. When I was a small boy there was a good chance that, on any fine summer's day in the school holidays, Auntie Jane would decide to take out a party of local children on a picnic. Off we would go packed like sardines into her little car to Bolton Abbey, Malham Tarn or just some quiet little spot which only she knew but which was nearly always by a stream or a pond or a river.

The picnic usually consisted of sandwiches, crisps, chocolate biscuits and apples, which were usually washed down with lemonade, Tizer or - best of all - Dandelion and Burdock. This feast was almost invariably laid out and enjoyed in a field full of buttercups and daisies.

Auntie Jane was the first to teach us children to make daisy chains (the last link in the chain always being the most difficult), and after we had made daisy chains we would hold buttercups under each other's chins and ask 'Do you like butter' - which of course we all did when the bright yellow was reflected upwards from the flowers. Under her supervision we would make and sail paper boats on whatever stretch of water lay close at hand, and she would delight in watching us feed the ducks with the remains of the picnic.

Being a botanist and naturalist, Auntie Jane's knowledge of country things extended way beyond buttercups and daisies. Being a teacher she encouraged us to talk and to ask questions, and she would often teasingly reply with little country rhymes and sayings.

'What's the difference between a weasel and a stoat?', one of us would ask.

'Well, dear', she would reply, 'a weasel is weasily distinguished from a stoat, which is stoatally different.'

Another would then ask: 'Please, Auntie Jane, what's the difference between a rook and a crow?'

She would smile before replying.

'Well, I always try to remember the difference this way, when a rook's on its own it's a crow and when a crow's in a crowd it's a rook.'

I think she deliberately designed her replies to excite our curiosity to learn.

I sometimes wonder whether there are any Auntie Janes still around these days to take small children on picnics, teach them to make daisy chains and to sail paper boats and to feed the ducks on the river.

Last of all, but by no means least, was Auntie Molly. My sister and I particularly looked forward to the visits of Auntie Molly. She would invariably just arrive, without notice or invitation, hotfoot from some exotic part of the world, but always looking glamorous in a beautiful flowery dress, wearing a broad brimmed hat and white gloves and glittering exquisite jewellery.

'Just passing through', she would say and then stay with us for a fortnight.

We loved seeing her, not simply because we admired her glamour and style, but because she was the most marvellous story teller. Her husband had been in the Indian Civil Service and she had spent a lot of time in the East. We sat at her feet enthralled as she spoke of the days of the Raj, and of glittering Governor's receptions, and we held our breath as she recounted tales of man-eating tiger hunts and long chases after giant blue butterflies in the Burmese jungle.

If Molly's life was one of glamour and adventure, she had also known sadness and tragedy. In less than two years she had lost her husband, brother and mother. But, undaunted, she carried on with her life, spending much more time travelling abroad and visiting her friends all over the world.

She possessed the enviable quality of being able to adapt easily to all manner of people and classes. She was at home dressed to the nines in a smart London hotel, but equally comfortable in the company of young people at a youth hostel. In Kipling's immortal words: 'She could walk with kings yet not lose the common touch.' Above all she retained a special affection and sympathy for the young, for she remained young at heart herself.

By the time I had become a solicitor, Auntie Molly was nearly seventy but she was still travelling the world. She kept in touch by sending me postcards, always written in the most beautiful descriptive prose making me feel I was there with her. Now she was staying with friends in Cyprus, then she was off to Paris for a few days, now travelling with a party of students in Mongolia, then skiing in Austria and so on.

Apart from being an intrepid traveller, delicious prose writer, fine skier, and a wonderful story teller, Auntie Molly was an excellent golfer and she once showed me a faded photograph of herself being presented with the Ladies Championship Cup at the Isle of Man tournament before the war.

When she stayed in England, which was never for very long, she lived in her gracious flat near the sea at Southport, and it was there, on one memorable occasion only, that I saw her golf swing in action.

I had gone over to Southport to discuss some matter of business with her and, after that had been happily concluded, she insisted that I accompany her on a tour of some of her favourite places in the resort. After walking along Lord Street with all its splendid shops and a brisk stroll along the pier and back, she was drawn, as if by a magnet, to the nearby pitch and putt course. There from the first tee I contrived a most awful attempted pitch shot which bumped along the ground and landed straight in the nearest bunker.

'Never mind, dear', she said sympathetically. 'You play tennis, don't you? Now just stand to the side and watch my swing.'

I stood back and watched first in admiration and then with anxiety as she launched into an almighty swing.

Molly had clearly forgotten that she was playing on a small seaside pitch and putt course, and had obviously imagined that she was driving off the championship course at Birkdale or St Andrew's. Her magnificently-struck drive sent the ball soaring skywards. Up, up and away it went, and I held my breath as it went way out of bounds. My anxiety turned to horror as I watched the ball eventually land right in the middle of a children's paddling pool. I raced to the edge of the pool. Mercifully none of the children had been hit, and there it was, one shiny golf ball right in the middle of the pool.

I have always known that golf - like beagling - is a rather complicated way of taking a walk, but until that moment I hadn't realised it could involve bathing as well. There was nothing else for it, so I took off my shoes and socks, rolled up my trousers and joined a number of rather puzzled-looking children in the paddling pool as I waded out rather sheepishly to retrieve the golf ball.

By this time Molly had arrived.

'We'll be alright now dear', she shouted across the paddling pool, 'I'll soon find my length now.'

I wasn't too anxious to find out whether Molly had now found her length, so I suggested we call it a day and have a cup of tea - or something a bit stronger.

Soon after my golf 'lesson' Molly died, and she died as she lived, in the midst of drama and adventure. She had collapsed with a heart attack on a London street and a nearby police car had picked her up to rush her to hospital. On the way to hospital the police car had a request from headquarters to intercept a car which had been involved in an armed bank robbery. The police in the car started to explain their predicament but Molly, who by this time had regained consciousness and could hear what was going on, absolutely insisted that they should do their duty. There followed a high-speed car chase through London with Molly, ill though she was, sitting in the back and enjoying every minute of it. The robbers were eventually caught, and when the police finally got Molly to hospital she just smiled at them and died. She wouldn't have wished it any other way for she died as she lived - bravely, adventurously and unselfishly.

Farmer's Glory

I am convinced that there are some people who are born survivors, and one of my favourite clients, May Beilby, was a living proof of this truth. She also demonstrated what I also believe to be true - namely that anything in this life that you really want to do or become you can achieve.

Ever since she had been a little girl, May had cherished the ambition of owning and running her own farm, but through a combination of circumstances this had never been possible. She had married young, had been ill herself with TB and then after recovering from that her husband had a stroke which left him semi-paralysed and in need of constant attention, a role which she selflessly fulfilled for many years.

She was fifty when her husband eventually died. He left her very little money and she had no experience of farming whatsoever, but the ambition she had retained since her childhood still burned as strongly as ever within her. As I cautioned her about the capital that would be required, the hard work that would be involved and the vagaries of the market, she shrugged her shoulders and said:

'It's what I've always wanted to do. It's now or never.'

So without further ado she sold her house and its contents, and with a few thousand pounds which she managed to beg and borrow she ploughed the lot into the purchase of a fifty acre smallholding just outside Denley. Her bank manager was aghast.

'Don't worry about him, John', she said, 'I've seen off three bank managers already and this one doesn't look as if he'll last very long!'

As for the local farmers, well, to say they were sceptical about her prospects would be a considerable understatement. Denley farmers undoubtedly possess many fine qualities, but they would hardly see themselves as being in the forefront of the women's liberation movement.

'T' lass 'll nobbut last t' year', said one of them, summing up their collective attitude.

May, totally undeterred by the dire warnings of her bank manager and only spurred on by the scepticism of the local farming community, threw herself single-mindedly into the work of a farmer, and started to build up a small dairy herd. Her needs were few, she had no family to support, but even so I did not really expect her to survive. I hardly dared contact her to see how she was doing, but I knew it must be a struggle because of the anxious telephone calls I was receiving at intervals from her bank manager.

Then after two years of bitter struggle, hard work and anxiety the breakthrough came. May came proudly smiling into my office one day to tell me that she had won first prize with one of her Herefords at the Great Yorkshire Show. This was the turning point and I found to my delight that the local farmers had now accepted her as one of them. Soon afterwards I happened to be at the local auction mart and there she was, sitting in glory surrounded by the same farmers who two years previously had been so sceptical and dismissive of her, but who were now actually competing with each other to buy her a pint of Tetley's.

'It looks like you've made it', I said to her. 'Congratulations.'

She just raised her glass in the air towards me and smiled.

'I Like to See a Good Fire'

'Tha wants a reet good fire at t' bottom, and then it'll burn for a fortneet', my old mentor Jacob used to say standing over me as I lit the bonfire in our garden at the back end of the year.

I know the gardening experts always tell us that it's a waste of good compost material to make a bonfire - and maybe they are right - but there are some things like rose prunings which don't decompose too quickly or easily, and anyway I like a bonfire. Or rather I like two bonfires, one in the spring and one in the autumn. I wouldn't be without an open fire in the sitting room either, for there's surely a comfort and a warmth in a real fire that you can never get from an artificial one, however realistic it may appear to be. My granny always claimed to be able to see faces and the shapes of animals in a coal fire, and to this day I cannot look into a fire without trying to see them.

I have also represented several clients who have been charged with arson, but it is only Billy Walter's case that I remember. Billy, who was 'ten t' dozen' as they say round here, was a young lad who was very easily led. When I defended him he had set fire to a mill and caused damage of more than £50,000.

'Why did you do it, Billy', I asked him. He went silent for a minute so I repeated my question.

'Well, you see Mr Francis, I like to see a good fire.'

'How on earth do you use that in mitigation?', I thought. The answer is that you don't.

'Can you argue better than borstal?', the trial judge asked my client's defending barrister. He couldn't and he didn't.

I was thinking about Billy's case as I stood over the dying embers of this autumn's bonfire. Because I'm an old-fashioned muck and magic gardener I cling to the belief that the ashes will be just the job to put around my gooseberry bushes and to help form the base for next year's spuds, a base which will help produce a crop to see the family safely through the following winter. When you really believe in something, its surprising how often it happens.

The Old Lag and the Denley Yob

I suppose all solicitors have their favourite criminal clients, and they are often the ones who are forever appearing before the courts, not just because, as some might cynically think, they are good for business but because their regular visits to the office make them so familiar that they become part of the furniture.

Derek Hattersley was the epitome of what used to be called 'an old lag'. Aged fifty-six, he had spent most of his life in institutions of one kind or another, graduating from approved schools to borstal and finally to prison. He seemed constitutionally and pathologically unable to stay out of trouble for longer than a few months and he was certainly the least proficient and most amateur criminal I have ever represented. This was not just because he was always or nearly always caught, but because he always instructed me to put forward the most unbelievable defences. If his story strained my credibility, I used to say to him, it would certainly have the same effect upon the court.

Derek was not a violent criminal, and indeed I cannot recall him ever being convicted for any crime of violence. His speciality was breaking and entering houses, warehouses and commercial premises. On being caught in a desirable residence one night, he told police he had been simply testing its security.

On another occasion upon being found on certain commercial premises in the town he insisted that he was only there out of curiosity. This was equally unconvincing in court.

But his most memorable 'defence' came in a case where he was committed for jury trial on a charge of breaking and entering a warehouse. His explanation was that he was suffering very badly from piles at the time and in a moment of desperation he had entered the warehouse in order to break wind! I also remember this case for the classic summing up by the prosecuting counsel which consisted of just one sentence:

'Members of the jury, are there fairies at the bottom of your garden?'

Back went Derek to prison again, which at least protected society from him - or vice-versa.

Kevin Murgatroyd, otherwise known as 'the Denley yob', was a different type of criminal client altogether, similar to Derek only in the regularity of his court appearances. He was the classic young tearaway. His specialities were fights, abusive behaviour, drunkenness, breaches of the peace and generally being involved in public disorders of one kind or another. He was aggressive, foul-mouthed and disrespectful of all authority. Denley folk said almost with one voice, 'He'll come to no good, that lad'.

I was, however, prepared to suspend judgement, for I had seen and known his type before. One of the main differences between solicitors and barristers is that the latter only see the client for the duration of a case, whereas solicitors have continued contact with their clients, sometimes over many years. It is interesting as well as surprising in some cases to observe how clients can change and develop.

Suddenly Kevin's court appearances stopped, and I didn't hear from him for a couple of years until one day he came into my office accompanied by a very pretty, sensible-looking girl, whom he introduced to me as his fiancée, and told me they were buying a home together. My impression that at long last Kevin was settling down was confirmed several years after that when he instructed me in the purchase of a business. The criminal client had graduated to a conveyancing client and now to a commercial client. I could only hope that he would not now be tempted to commit a criminal act of commercial fraud to make the circle complete!

From All Corners of the Office

Insult to Injury

It is not just the colourful clients and friends who come to the office who provide interest in the life of a practising solicitor, for it is often necessary for a solicitor to visit them in their own homes. This can sometimes be a rather unproductive and time-consuming business. After a conducted tour of the house, a long conversation on matters of health, weather and the state of the country followed by a detailed perusal of the family album, the actual business is eventually discussed, but often ends with the client saying something like, 'Well, thank you very much, Mr Francis, there's a lot for me to think about, isn't there?' No wonder solicitors always have files full of unfinished business.

There was one occasion, however, when the procedure I have described was interrupted in a totally unexpected fashion. I had gone to see old Mrs Prothero, who always expected me to visit her at her bungalow and who wished to discuss changing her will for the umpteenth time.

We were in her beautifully appointed lounge, the kind of room where nothing was out of place and where one hardly dared sit down for fear of ruffling a cushion. For over half an hour she described her various medical ailments in vivid and excruciating detail, and for the next half hour she told me in highly emotional terms of her daughter's marriage problems. Luckily I found it rather hard to hear everything she said because Jimmy Ainsworth, the local joiner, was working in the loft space above the room.

Suddenly, just as I was wondering whether my client wouldn't be better talking to a doctor or a marriage counsellor, there was an almighty crash and we both looked up to see Jimmy plunge straight through the ceiling and land on the floor right next to us. Jimmy was bruised, cut, shocked and shaken but fortunately he did not seem to be too badly hurt.

Poor old Mrs Prothero, however, on seeing the state of her room, the dust and the debris, Jimmy lying on the floor with blood trickling onto the carpet, went quite hysterical. I made her sit down and fetched a bottle of brandy from her cocktail cabinet. After she and Jimmy had both had a glass of brandy they felt better, but I suggested to Jimmy that I had better take him to casualty just to make sure nothing was broken.

When the doctor had completed his examination he asked if he could have a word with me in private.

'I've given your friend a thorough examination, Mr Francis. There's nothing broken and apart from cuts and bruises he seems fine. But, has he been drinking?'

'Oh dear,' I thought.

I told him about the brandy I had given him after the accident but I'm not sure whether he believed me. Later I took Jimmy home and told him what had happened. Considering

the possible damage I had done to his reputation as a sober workman, I was rather surprised when he asked me a couple of days later to become his solicitor. Whenever we met after that, I would always greet him with, 'Now then Jimmy, have you been drinking?' One of these days I think he might hit me but so far he has just laughed.

As for Mrs Prothero, when I went back to make sure she was alright after I had taken Jimmy to hospital I found that she was far more concerned about Jimmy than the damage to her lounge. I reassured her that, apart from being badly shocked and having some cuts and bruises, no serious damage had been done.

'I always say, Mr Francis, that when there's an accident, the only thing that really matters is that nobody has been hurt.'

When I meet people like that it rekindles my faith in human nature.

He Who Laughs Last

Practising law is, on the whole, a serious business. So serious in fact that it is all too easy to lose one's sense of proportion as well as one's sense of humour. Fortunately there are always a few clients who help their solicitor to retain both.

Conveyancing, contrary to popular myth, is arguably the most fraught, anxiety-inducing and difficult part of a solicitor's work. Certainly an advocate has to apply himself more to strictly legal issues and has to be able to think and argue on his feet, but I think I have had more sleepless nights over conveyancing transactions than ever I had over any court case. There are, amongst many other things, searches to be made, enquiries and requisitions on title to be raised, contracts to be drafted and gone through with a fine-toothed comb, mortgages to be arranged and prepared, completion dates to be agreed and all the administration to be organised so that transactions, sometimes forming only part of a large chain, can fall into place.

In the Dales, property sales are often beset by problems over boundaries, rights of way, septic tanks and - often as not - missing deeds. I once complained to an elderly Dales solicitor of some defect in his client's deeds, and he gave me very short shrift indeed.

'You should count yourself lucky, young man, that my client's got a packet of title deeds at all', he said.

It's not so bad dealing with solicitors who know the problems, but dealing with city firms who do not can be hell. There was one case where I was acting for a farmer in the sale of some land to a purchaser who instructed a particularly arrogant and pompous London solicitor to act on his behalf.

He was as difficult and awkward throughout the transaction as it is possible to imagine, possibly because he was accustomed to handling residential and commercial conveyances rather than sales of agricultural land. So when the day of completion finally arrived, he telephoned and said in his most patronising and affected manner:

'Tell me, Mr Francis, what arrangements have you put in hand to effect a transfer of the keys?'

It gave me considerable satisfaction to be able to give him the direct reply:

'We don't lock up land in Yorkshire.'

Moving house is undoubtedly one of the biggest, most important and sometimes most traumatic experience in anyone's life, so all the detailed work a solicitor has to do is carried out against a background of anxious vendors and purchasers, who more and more these days regrettably seek to manoeuvre the transaction to their own advantage and pursue their own interests without considering the position of others involved in the chain.

Acting for friends and relatives in a conveyancing transaction can be particularly tricky, partly because they tend to assume that they are free to telephone at any time of day or night to discuss the minutiae of the transaction and also because if anything at all goes wrong you feel particularly vulnerable. They also sometimes have a wicked, nay perverted, sense of humour.

Bill and Monica Evans had been good family friends for many years and I had acted for them on their last house move. It was a fraught transaction, but completion was eventually achieved and I was satisfied that I had done a reasonably good job.

About a couple of months afterwards, Rosemary and I were invited to their new house for dinner. After a few pleasantries had been exchanged, Bill suddenly became serious.

'John', he said, 'you never told me about the right of way our neighbours have through our back garden. They can look straight in at us through the kitchen window.'

Bill's delivery was perfect, his expression deadpan. Rosemary told me later that at that moment I literally turned white in the face. I had been so completely taken in that, even after Bill told me he was joking, I needed more than one drink to recover.

For six months afterwards I bided my time as I plotted revenge. I got a friend of mine at the local council to let me have a blank form of notice to acquire property under a compulsory purchase order, and then typed it to the effect that Bill's property was to be the subject of a compulsory purchase order as it was considered unfit for human habitation. I then posted it by recorded delivery.

I knew Bill had been taken in when he rang me in a panic to seek advice on the 'notice' he had received from the council. He had clearly forgotten his little joke on me and sounded badly shaken.

'The council can't do this to us, can they? What's wrong with the house anyway? I don't understand it.'

I paused.

'Well Bill, I reckon it's a bit like that right of way through your back garden. I think that makes us all square.'

There was a long pause before Bill said, 'Well, you rotten bastard.'

There was another pause before he laughed and then we both laughed. A Solicitor of the Supreme Court and Commissioner for Oaths I may be but I remain, I think, a boy still at heart.

Where There's a Will

During my years in practice I have drawn up countless wills, and I think solicitors are generally very pleased when their clients decide to have their wills professionally drafted. I have seen many 'home-made' wills, and I wish I had been given a pound for every invalid one, for I would be a wealthy man by now. Many members of the general public have found to their cost the truth of the old adage: 'Home-made will, solicitor's bill'.

There is, in my experience, widespread ignorance concerning the rules governing wills and intestacy. There is for instance no presumption in law that children have to be treated equally in a will, and in the absence of testamentary incapacity, duress or undue influence (all notoriously difficult to prove) the testator's will must stand, subject only to the right of dependents to claim against the estate under the Inheritance Family Provision Acts.

In a case I had some years ago, a widowed father left all his estate to his daughter who had spent many years looking after him following his wife's death, and made no provision whatsoever for his son. Now his son thought this was most unfair as he had done nothing to offend his father, had achieved all the goals in life his father had set him and had built up a successful and flourishing business.

I had to remind him that life isn't always fair and that to contest the will would almost certainly prove fruitless and that if unsuccessful he would have heavy costs to pay. I could not resist quoting to him the old rhyme:

'For a dutiful son, it is sad to relate

That he only got costs from his father's estate.'

A will is, in fact, a highly technical document, and too often home-made wills either lack essential legal requirements, like not being properly witnessed or, because of the inadequate or ambiguous wording used, fail to implement the real wishes of the testator. For this reason, solicitors in the past have charged very little for making wills simply to encourage their clients to have them properly made. For many years my own firm charged the princely sum of one guinea for this service.

The subject is, however, a tricky one to raise with a client. Many people still tend to regard a will as 'a remembrancer of death' and invent all sorts of excuses for putting off making one. I should not care to be too censorious on this point, however, as solicitors are notoriously bad at putting their own affairs in order and have been known to die intestate themselves!

I have made wills for clients in all sorts of different places, at home, at the office, at hotels, at farms - even on holiday - but surely one of the saddest and most difficult tasks a solicitor has to perform is to see a client to make a will in hospital or an old people's home.

Some of these homes are splendidly run but there are others I have visited where I have found my client sitting in the middle of a large semi-circle of old folk huddled round a fire, all looking dejected and bored, with only the next meal to look forward to, and all apparently simply waiting to die. In such circumstances the visit of a solicitor tends to be the object of a certain morbid curiosity.

There have been some such occasions when the matron or the proprietor of the home has taken me on one side and expressed anxiety about the number of relatives who have suddenly started to descend to see my client like vultures circling before a death. The old tend to become very vulnerable to suggestion, particularly by those upon whom they depend in one way or another. This is a good reason for making a will early in life. Solicitors know better than most that wills and death seem often to bring out the worst in people and that where there's a will . . . there's relatives!

There are, thankfully, many old people who remain fully active, independent and in full possession of their faculties. They are the ones to be envied.

Two of my favourite clients were Annie and Jessie Collier, elderly sisters who lived in a little old cottage on the outskirts of Denley. I once visited them in their home to take instructions on proposed codicils to their wills. At that time Annie was ninety-six years of age and her younger sister Jessie was ninety-three. After our business had been concluded they insisted I stayed for what proved to be a magnificent tea complete with crumpets and home-made raspberry jam and cakes.

Annie then took me quietly on one side and, after making a series of complaints about her younger sister's general behaviour, she said:

'But I mustn't be too hard on her, must I, Mr Francis. I really do think that ninety-three is a very difficult age in the life of a woman, don't you?'

Lawyers are not by their nature and occupation often stuck for words, but on this occasion I must confess I was completely stumped. As the late and much-lamented Eric Morecambe would have said: 'There's no answer to that!'

Nobody Knew She Was There

All sorts of different people came to our office - and I don't just mean clients. There are bank and building society managers making courtesy calls, office equipment and stationery salesmen, insurance brokers and financial services advisers and representatives of various local charities, schools and voluntary bodies looking for contributions towards their particular cause. But there was one instance when a visitor to our office premises stayed rather longer than she had intended.

As I was working away in my office drafting some agreements I became aware of a noise which seemed to come from outside the building, but as there were some workmen doing some pointing to the outside walls I took little notice of it at first. However, the knocking noise became louder and more insistent, to the point where I decided to go outside to investigate.

I then discovered that the noise was coming from our gents toilet door. I realised that there was a woman evidently locked in it who was becoming completely hysterical. The door turned out not to be locked but jammed. I shouted to the woman to stand back and I eventually managed to ease it open. An elderly woman I had never seen before in my life collapsed into my arms, but I assumed her to be a client who had probably just got lost.

'I'm so sorry about this', I said, 'can I offer you a cup of coffee?'

'I think I need something stronger', she sobbed.

It transpired that the good lady was not a client at all but an ordinary member of the public. Doing her shopping she suddenly realised that she was in urgent need of the toilet. The nearest public toilets were quite some way away so she had simply come off the street to use ours. In her hurry and desperation she had mistaken the gents for the ladies.

'We really must get that door fixed', I said at the next partners' meeting. 'Another time it might be one of our clients who is locked in there.'

'Not necessarily a bad thing', replied one of my partners. 'It's one way of retaining our clients.'

I think he was joking.

The Wine Merchant Cometh

Amongst the regular visitors to our office is a certain wine merchant, for it is perhaps not a surprising fact that solicitors like other professional people tend to be targeted by the wine trade. Now my staff are all well trained to shield me from unwanted calls by reps of one kind or another, but they have always had a standing instruction from me to make an exception in the case of the wine merchant on the basis that a wine sampling session makes a most pleasant and welcome change from the day's routine appointments. It can, however, have its disadvantages too.

There was one occasion when the appointment with the wine merchant lasted rather longer than I had intended, and the number and the variety of wines I sampled were considerably greater than usual. The problem, if such it can be called, of tasting a number of different vintage wines is that you tend to lose track of how much you are actually drinking and also their potency.

This was my first mistake, and by the time I had gone through the salesman's entire list my desk resembled a cocktail bar at closing time and I was feeling rather happy with life in general. My second mistake after the wine merchant had gone was to attempt to give some shorthand dictation to a member of staff. The member of staff I selected for this doubtful privilege was Miss Beaumont, she who for over forty years had been the uncrowned conveyancing queen of Denley, she who had seen countless partners and solicitors come and go and knew more about solicitors and the workings of a solicitors' office than I would ever learn in a lifetime

I made several somewhat incoherent attempts at dictating a letter, interrupted by hiccups and giggles.

'Er, dear shir, I mean madam' - hiccup - 'with refererence to your letter of the firtieth of May concerning your hoving mouse' - giggle - 'I just want to say - oh hell, that's not right is it, Miss Beaumont. Erm, I have to advishe you.'

I noticed that Miss Beaumont was looking at me intently. She spoke for the first time.

'Do you think it would be a good idea if we try again a bit later, Mr Francis?', she said as she got up and left the office.

She went out quickly and I could see that she was having some difficulty in keeping a straight face.

The Bench, The Bar and The Long Arm of The Law

I have told at length and in some detail of the various clients, characters and friends who have impinged on my life as a country solicitor, and of others who have been part of my practice, but no portrait of a country solicitor - or indeed any solicitor - would be complete without some reference being made to those other servants of the law, the police, the barristers and the judges.

Magistrates courts used to be known as police courts, and when I first started appearing in them as an advocate I felt very aware of that historical fact. For one thing, most of the prosecutions in those days were not only initiated and prepared by the police but were actually conducted in court by a police officer, usually an inspector or superintendent. For another thing I was often conscious, whether justifiably or not, of a relationship between police and magistrates which seemed to reveal an identity of feeling and purpose.

This feeling was reinforced in one of my early cases when I applied to the magistrates for an adjournment to a particular date. The chairman of the bench turned to the chief superintendent who was appearing for the prosecution and said:

'Is that alright with us, chief superintendent?'

About the same time there was also a story in circulation of a young, very learned solicitor who at the close of evidence addressed the magistrates at some length. He laid emphasis on a number of matters which suggested that there was a doubt in the case and that it was the task of the prosecution to prove the case against his client beyond reasonable doubt. At the close of his submission the chairman of the bench, a blunt, down-to-earth Yorkshireman, said to him:

'We do find that theer's a doubt in this case, but we're not goin' to give t' benefit of it to thee, we're givin' it to t' police instead.'

Nowadays things are, of course, very different. Police no longer conduct prosecutions and magistrates are better trained and much more professional in their approach. For all that the judicial process has been improved by these changes, I must confess to missing some of the wily and experienced police officers with whom I used to do battle in court, and some of the colourful characters who used to sit on the magistrates bench.

When I speak of the police I must, though, declare an interest, for one of my most inspiring mentors as a boy was my grandfather, who was a very senior and distinguished police officer. Nothing that has happened to me as a solicitor has altered my view that we have a police force in this country which is the best in the world.

Many members of the public still think of a barrister as a superior type of lawyer to a solicitor, a view that, in the past at any rate, some barristers by their attitude and style have tended to reinforce.

Certainly when I first qualified, many members of the bar seemed to regard themselves as the only gentlemen left! In truth, it is easier to qualify as a barrister than as a solicitor and the only substantive differences are that a barrister at present enjoys an exclusive right of audience in the higher courts and that he cannot accept instructions direct from a client but only through a solicitor - though these restrictions are liable to change in the near future.

Barristers range from those who inhabit the rarified world of the chancery bar to the much more down-to-earth criminal 'briefs'. They even have their own language. I was once representing a tenant in a case before the Agricultural Lands Tribunal and the landlord was represented by a barrister. The day before the hearing, the barrister had not finished a case in which he was defending five men who were jointly charged with committing rape, so a telephone call was made to the secretary of the tribunal to ask for an adjournment as he was 'still part-heard in a five-handed rape'. I suspect that that worthy civil servant is still trying to get his mind round that particular concept. He was certainly puzzled by it at the time.

To a general practitioner like myself, access to a barrister is essential from time to time, sometimes to obtain specialist advice on a question to which he doesn't know the answer, to represent a client in a higher court or simply to obtain a second opinion. There are certain cases and certain clients where the assistance of counsel is absolutely invaluable. There have been times, however, when I have taken a client to see counsel in conference and the results have not been what I expected.

There was one such occasion where I took a client of mine, a redoubtable old Dales farmer named Harry Waterhouse, to see a barrister to advise on whether he had the legal right to graze his sheep on an adjoining fell, a right he thought he had but which was now in dispute.

Learned counsel sat in a dark pinstriped suit and gold watch chain behind a massive oak desk piled high with bundles of documents tied with pink ribbons known as briefs.

'Mr Waterhouse, I have had the opportunity of considering the papers in this case and I have to advise you that there are six possible methods of acquiring easements, which we must examine in turn and then consider to what extent they apply to profits à prendre.'

Already out of the corner of my eye I could see Harry's jaw slowly dropping and his expression was one of bafflement and disbelief.

'There is statute, express grant, implied grant, presumption at common law, lost modern grant and the Prescription Act of 1932.'

Counsel then went on to give an erudite dissertation on these topics, and also by way of bonus told my client something of the law regarding 'equitable estoppel', a concept which I guessed was none too familiar to Harry in his daily life on the farm. I must admit that I myself had some difficulty following his detailed and complex reasoning.

Counsel than turned to me:

'Section sixty-two of the Law of Property Act is your answer, Mr Francis. The decision in White versus Williams in 1922 applies. I don't think I can assist you further. Good afternoon, gentlemen.'

With that he picked up the bundle of papers from his desk and walked quickly out.

Harry turned to me. His expression of incomprehension had by this time turned to one of total bewilderment.

'Nay, Mr Francis, what the bloody 'ell were all that about? I could 'ave gitten more sense out o' one o' me yows - an' a damn sight cheaper an' all!'

'It means you're alright, Harry. You can put your sheep on that fell, and if anyone tells you differently you tell him you've got White versus Williams in 1922 on your side. You might like to mention equitable estoppel just for good measure. He may think you know something he doesn't!'

It is from the ranks of barristers that our judges are mainly appointed - though I am pleased to say not exclusively so. There are a few ex-solicitors on the bench and very well most of them seem to be doing. The appointment of more experienced solicitors as judges can only in my opinion be a good thing.

Not that I have ever myself craved for a judicial appointment, for being a judge calls for very special abilities and qualities. It is a most difficult job, at times a lonely one and one where you are constantly under scrutiny and liable to criticism from press and public. I believe that most judges are lawyers of considerable ability and experience. The general public expect that, but they also look for courtesy, consideration and the ability to provide a fair hearing. I have come across judges who fully measure up to all these expectations, but there is unfortunately in my experience a too-large category of judges who suffer from a condition well known in the legal profession as 'judgitis'. It is a condition which seems to afflict a large number of lawyers the minute they are appointed judges and their bottoms hit the bench. The symptoms of the condition are arrogance, pomposity, impatience and rudeness.

It perhaps does not matter too much when judges direct strong criticism in open court at solicitors, even if they generally have no knowledge whatever of the pressure and problems in a solicitor's office and even if such criticisms are sometimes made on the basis of incomplete facts. After all, lawyers are paid for doing court work, and a rude tirade from a judge whether justified or not can be said to be part of the job.

What in my view is totally inexcusable is rudeness from a judge directed towards vulnerable and anxious members of the public. Lawyers in general and judges in particular frequently fail to realise what an ordeal it is for many people to have to appear at court - let alone to step into the witness box and give evidence.

Nowadays, thank goodness, most divorce cases do not require evidence to be given in open court, but for many years they did and I have never forgotten the rudeness, sarcasm and lack of sympathy which was often directed by judges to already very nervous female petitioners when they were trying to give evidence, sometimes about the most intimate details of their married life.

Judges, like the police, barristers and solicitors, are not perfect but what we all share is the privilege of serving a judicial process which is independent of government, a rarity if you look around most of the countries of the world.

The Trouble With Being A Solicitor

One of the troubles with being a solicitor is that you tend to pick up committees like confetti, for it seems to be thought 'a good thing' to have a solicitor as chairman of this organisation and secretary of that committee.

Certainly any solicitor worth his salt should be prepared to serve and be involved in the community where he lives and works, but if he is not careful he can very quickly and easily find himself being immersed in legal work in a disproportionate part of his limited spare time.

Drafting constitutions and advising on legal aspects of business meetings may be worthy and necessary jobs which have to be done by someone, but they are hardly what most solicitors would choose to do outside the office. Acting for and professionally advising a club or voluntary organisation is usually difficult enough anyway. If there is a constitution in existence you tend to find that it has been drawn up in about 1867 by a complete amateur, has not seen the light of day since and does not cover the point at issue. There's another problem when you are acting for clubs; their officials are always either dying, resigning or leaving the district, so you rarely know from week to week with which official you are dealing.

Whisper it ever so quietly but often the most successful long-term tactic for a solicitor attempting to resolve problems at clubs and societies is to engage in what is known throughout the profession as 'masterly inactivity'. I know that our critics among the general public believe we engage in this most of the time as a matter of course. I would protest that this is not true, but I would also cheerfully concede it to be a most useful tactic in certain cases, particularly where litigation involving clubs and societies is involved. Many litigants will give up eventually and many problems, particularly the ones you worry about most will, if the matter is left for long enough, solve themselves.

I used to help with the running of a local village hall where the trustees were two particularly awkward old men. They instructed me to take legal action against a former trustee over the most trivial of matters. Any litigation would have soon split the village in two, so I kept telling them again and again that I needed more time to research the legal documents. Eventually one of them died and the other followed him to the grave not long afterwards. Death solves many problems!

Quite apart from being regarded as a natural for committee work, it is also commonly assumed that because you are a solicitor you will automatically, and without any preparation whatsoever, be able to make a brilliant, original and witty after-dinner speach at a moment's notice. Regrettably this is not always the case.

There is a well-known story told about the late Sir Norman Birkett KC (as he then was), one of my boyhood heroes. Birkett was one of the very few men I know of ever to have made any money out of the law - and most of that was made out of broadcasting after his retirement! He was attending a dinner and sitting next to a solicitor who rose to make a speech. The solicitor's speech went unexpectedly badly. He stuttered and stumbled, he couldn't find the right words and his jokes fell flat. The harder he tried, the worse he got, his face reddened and he started to perspire profusely. All in all it was a total disaster. Eventually he sat down with a sigh of relief, mopped his brow and turned to Birkett.

'If you'd been making that speech how would you have gone about it?'

As quick as a flash Birkett replied:

'If I'd have been you, I'd have made that speech under an assumed name!'

But it does remain a popular fallacy that lawyers can be relied upon to make the best after-dinner speeches. I have myself heard some appalling speeches by solicitors, barristers and even by High Court judges. There are a few, and only a few, who possess the gift of making brilliant speeches readily and effortlessly. They may be lawyers or they may not.

The majority of good speeches - whether by lawyers or non-lawyers - will almost certainly be as the result of thoughtful and careful preparation, but the lawyer's preparation has to be extra thoughtful and extra careful because more is expected of him. The conclusion must be that whenever a lawyer makes a speech, he is on a hiding to nothing. If he is successful it's only what is expected of someone in his profession and if he fails, well that's a bad show for someone in his job, isn't it?

The Times They Are A-Changing

People were always remarking when I was growing up that 'there aren't the characters about these days that there used to be', and I tended to believe this until I became a solicitor.

That is not to say that my practice is fully taken up with colourful clients, interesting cases and amusing incidents, for that is only part of the picture. There is also much that is tedious, much that is repetitive, much that is routine and there is the telephone - always the telephone.

Perhaps it is true that there's no peace for the wicked, or as my Scottish granny used to say, 'these things are sent to try us'. But if there is stress and anxiety every day there is also nearly always something to laugh about or something new to learn either about the law or about human beings.

For surely there can be nobody more aware of the enormous contrasts of the human condition than a country solicitor. In the morning he can be standing in the sunshine outside a farmhouse admiring anew the timeless beauty of the Dales, yet in the afternoon he can be seeing a client in a terminal cancer ward. Life can be so marvellous and yet with so many problems just in Denley and its surrounding villages. I reflect on how much human misery there must be in the world and how many people there must be who, as Thoreau put it, lead lives of 'quiet desperation'. I have noticed too that it invariably seems to be those who suffer most who complain least.

If I am put on the spot, I am not altogether sure what I would say has given me the most pleasure and satisfaction in my work, but I think I would say that it has to be either the winning of a difficult court case against the odds, or else the resolution of a seemingly intractable problem when I can both sense and see an intolerable burden lifting from my client's shoulders as he walks from my office out of the shadows and into the sunshine.

So, whither the country solicitor? A leading article in a national newspaper discussing recent changes in the legal profession described the traditional picture of a family solicitor as 'a gentleman in late middle age dressed in a tweed suit who gives good advice to clients in times of trouble'. I certainly do not yet admit to being in late middle age, but I do recognise the type described and I am by no means the only one to observe that he is rapidly becoming an endangered species.

A solicitor writing in a legal publication recently asked what will happen when the partners in the ordinary small firms of solicitors have retired or died and who is going to replace them. It is a good question but before I lament the present, wax sentimental about the past and start quoting Edward Thomas's 'Can I forget the sweet days that have been', I must remind myself that in every age there always have been and always will be people who will say that 'things ain't what they used to be, the morals of the young are deeply shocking and the country is going to the dogs'.

For what it's worth I reckon there is good and bad in every age and I do not myself believe that human nature changes very much from one generation to another. There can be no doubt however that the times they are a-changing, and I know from personal experience that this is especially true where solicitors and the Dales are concerned.

The solicitor who is a man of affairs, general practitioner and friend of the family is one of a dying breed - if he is still to be found at all. All the younger lawyers seem to be going into paid employment of some kind or they are joining the lucrative large commercial firms in the cities. I see professionalism, friendship and courtesy being replaced by commercialism and specialisation.

The new-style solicitors are hard-nosed, aggressive and competitive in their approach, and have adopted the business ethos to the point where I hear that some of them now have monthly targets just like sales representatives. It is therefore hardly surprising that many of them appear not so much interested in what they can do for their clients but how much they can charge them.

The future of the traditional family solicitor is also threatened by the banks, building societies and other large institutions. They now apparently wish to be conveyancers and probate experts as well as being estate agents, insurance brokers and moneylenders!

Although they would never admit it, the large city firms are clearly much more interested in their rich commercial and corporate clients than the man or woman in the street who, if they are taken on as clients at all, will probably never deal with the same solicitor twice, will probably not be seen by a partner and will be shunted around the office from one so-called specialist to another depending on the nature of the matter in hand.

As one of the last of the all-rounders I suppose I must declare an interest, but I think there are at least two reservations about the all-pervading growth of legal 'experts' and specialists, besotted as they are with their computers, fax machines, word processors and all their other modern gadgetry. The first is quite simply that they often get it wrong, and the second is that they have arguably much too narrow a perspective and experience to develop a 'feel' for a case.

The general practitioner will often by virtue of his breadth of experience of law and of life be in a much better position to advise a client whether a particular transaction is right for him or not, and he will almost certainly be able to impart sympathy and understanding to a widow in a probate case or emotional support to a petitioner going through a divorce which a so-called specialist, however much of a legal eagle he or she may be, and however much technical expertise he or she may have, simply cannot provide. Specialists have their place, but whereas you can always get technical advice you can't buy wisdom and humanity.

The times are a-changing too in the Dales towns and villages. Here too commercialism is spreading with the tawdry aspects of the tourist trade, theme parks, 'tarted-up' pubs and unsightly developments.

The old ways of farming are going. At a time when there are those who take the view that any farm under two hundred and fifty acres is not viable and should amalgamate with another I fear for the future of our Dales farmers and smallholders. These fears are heightened when all over the country I see the land increasingly passing from yeoman farming families, who have always regarded it as a sacred trust, into the hands of the institutions, the investment companies and the agri-businessmen who regard it as just another commodity to be bought and sold and to be exploited for maximum profit.

I fear too for the future of our small towns and villages when I see the way in which the architects, planners, civil servants, council officials, speculators, developers and bureaucrats have destroyed the beauty and the heart of many of our cities.

Amidst all the change of the past quarter of the century I have found pleasure and satisfaction in just being a country solicitor, but heartsease I have always found outside the law. For me it is and always has been since boyhood enjoying the simple pleasures of life. Seeing the first lambs, orange-tip butterflies and violets of early spring, playing a game of tennis on a summer evening, smelling new-mown hay and hearing the call of the curlew. Watching the heather moors taking their colour in August, getting the garden squared up at the back end and having a good bonfire. Putting my feet up by a log fire on a winter's night with one of my favourite country books. Going to Denley Show and hearing once again the talk of farmers and keepers. Observing the pageant of the changing seasons in the dale and above all just relaxing with the family at home. For in the end, surely, the family is all.

When I look at my family I find it difficult to believe how quickly the children have grown up. All parents have to realise sooner or later that they are just trustees for a time. My oldest son is now at university and, dare I admit it, working harder than I ever did as a student. My daughter is studying for her A-levels and my youngest son is just approaching the age of twelve, which I described on the very first page of this book as being a marvellous age for a boy.

At my side and at the heart of the family is their mother Rosemary, the same delightful girl I first knew all those years ago when she sold her baby budgies to the local pet shop, who has been sufficiently tolerant and long-suffering to be the wife of a country solicitor.

Before we were ever married we used to go out with her lovely English pointer called Sadie on long country walks and we talked together about our many shared interests and the sort of life we both wanted. Through all the ups and downs of a busy married life neither of us has ever lost our love of the countryside or our sense of wonder at the magic of nature. The things which delighted us both as children still do.

When, as is our habit, we take our dog out at dusk for an evening walk in the summer, there is old Bufo the toad, my friend in the garden, emerging by the gate, I am quite convinced, to greet me personally. As we walk on down the lane, the bats are flying, the owls are hooting and the sky already twinkles with a myriad of stars. Below us is the sound of the river, the air is soft and fragrant and the lights going on in the cottages remind us that 'the night cometh when no man can work'.

It is I think during these quiet special moments, when you are at one with nature, in tune with the rhythms of the season and the weather and happy within your family that you feel a link with the infinite and the eternal and are most likely to experience true spiritual contentment and peace of mind. When I look at my wife at such times I think how beautifully Coleridge expressed my own feelings when he wrote:

'The two divinest things the world has got,
A lovely woman in a rural spot.'

So far as the law is concerned I should very much like to think that the family solicitor will continue for some time yet to provide advice, friendship and sometimes a helping hand to his clients and to his local community. I fear, though, that as a species he is gradually disappearing and may soon be gone altogether, gone with the small shopkeepers, the men with moleskin waistcoats and the dark-green fritillaries and cowslip meadows of my boyhood.

On balance, however, my hopes just about overcome my fears and I remain stubbornly optimistic. I base my optimism on what I see to be a continuing need for the independent advice and personal service a family solicitor can provide. He is also perhaps the kind of person the Dalesfolk still prefer to turn to in time of trouble.

Whatever happens in the future to the legal profession and to its practitioners there are some things, the important things, which have not changed and which I trust and believe will never change. I refer of course to the abiding qualities of the Yorkshire Dalesfolk, their humanity and their humour, their integrity, their kindness and their friendship.

I often wonder why it is that we Tykes retain such a strong and special affinity to our county. It is certainly nothing new, for as long ago as 1682, Dr George Hickes, sometime Dean of Worcester, said in his sermon at the Yorkshire Feast in London:

'Our county, as the curious observe, is the Epitome of England; whatsoever is excellent in the whole land being to be found in proportion thereto . . . besides God hath been pleased to make it the birthplace and nursery of many great men.'

I only know that as a country solicitor, living amongst my own people and working for them, I have been blessed indeed.